Logic Jam

Unlocking the Value of Information

Edward J. Morawski

ISBN   978-1-4357-1739-8

Dedicated to my Children

Edward

Pamela

Michael

And

Grandchildren

Aaron

Brooke

Jessie

Shaun

Contents

Introduction

Many years of grappling with information in many different arenas has culminated in this effort to summarize the approach, process and skills I use regularly to manage a glut of information coming in from all directions in an "Information Age." From time to time a flood of information becomes like a log jam in a river. When this happens it disables our ability to do proper analysis and take decisive action. This "Logic Jam" requires we use some rather basic tools and diligent effort to restore normal thought processes allowing us to unlock the value of information once again.

You will find that the challenges you experience managing and using information aren't unique. The education and skills you need are basic and available to anyone. Glance through the *Occupational Outlook Handbook* by the US Department of Labor Bureau of Labor Statistics March 2004 and review the education and training requirements for any of the current jobs or jobs of tomorrow. You will

Introduction

quickly come to the realization that the information management skills although not referenced are key to acquiring the qualifications for the professions and jobs of today and tomorrow. Whether you acquire what you need to know through the internet, an audio file, a video file, a book or a lecture it is all information that requires your personal management.

We all share habits and practices that get us into trouble when the information starts to flow. Likewise, we all share a capacity for handling it once we have seen a common sense approach. Topics that are important to consider include:

- Preparing to process information
    - Developing a mindset
    - Tools and techniques
- Engaging the presenter or information source
    - Information management skills
- Analysis of key information
    - Organization and Flow
    - Critical Thinking
- Sorting information
- Storing information for future reference
- Presenting information
- Learning from experience
- Considering the Frontier

While working in a variety of jobs I found that managing information was always part of the work. There were times presenters or sources that didn't initially drown me with information made it difficult to stay afloat when they went into detail later. Having survived many assaults by those who would sedate me with text, audio, video, and dialogue, I would like to share what I have learned over the years in the hope that others may have an easier time of it.

Even though, certain technology may simplify things as is documented by David Thornburg in his book *The New Basics: Education and the Future of Work in the Telematic* Age written in 2002. The place any individual starts is some place in the mist of a life surrounded by information coming in from all sides. While confused by some information, most of us cope with this flood of information in one way or another.

I would suggest what is needed has less to do with gadgets and more to do with you. People with ability to engage and manage information generally will use technology, but technology is secondary to a useful mindset and management skills. Although, our lives may be totally different we have something in common when it comes to information.

CHAPTER 1

Why Should this Stuff Interest Me?

Having an edge over anyone that might compete for your job or business customers is a primary reason to sharpen your awareness and skills. Even in good times, employers and customers are interested in getting the most for their dollar. One of the factors that all customers recognize is "Perceived Quality" as detailed by Bradley T. Gale in *Managing Customer Value* 1994. Bradley T. Gale mentions information and analysis early in his book in my opinion, because its importance cannot be overlooked. Although the subject of *Managing Customer Value* doesn't focus on the individual ability to manage information, the person that manages information well tends not to miss details and secondary considerations employers and customers perceive as quality. It is a quality they may expect, but don't necessarily ask for specifically. You may be an employee, an employer or even a retiree all of which will need to manage information. If you produce goods and services or consume goods and services, you need to manage information. At some level how well you

Chapter 1. Why should this stuff interest me?

manage information will impact your finances.

Understand that the "Information Age" started a while ago and not just with the invention of the personal computer. People have been struggling with the management of information for a long time, and the extent of their struggle usually depended on what type of work they did. Some work is heavily dependent on information while other types still require only minimal pieces of information. If you either hold a job that requires you perform well in a crush of information or are considering such a career you will find what follows of interest. Doctors, lawyers, automotive technicians, school teachers, engineers, scientists, stock brokers, and computer programmers are all people that live under a crush of information, and not all manage it well. Instead, we are at different levels of understanding and ability, because some of us have been battling information overload for years while others are just learning what a mind numbing experience it can be.

You may have heard that information is valuable. If that is true then unlocking the value from information is an ability that many jobs and professions require to make them of value in the marketplace. Information is a raw material and like any raw material the value of information changes as it is made a part of some final product or service. As you read ask yourself, does this help me unlock value from information? Developing fundamental skills and understanding that can be applied to all information will enable you to be a more valuable commodity. Well paid people are usually thought of as smart at the very least. These people many times are expected to work without an

Chapter 1. Why should this stuff interest me?

instruction book. The people that know how to extract value from information are sought after regardless of the other work they do, because they seem to make sense of nonsense. These same people serve as an example of how repackaging information adds a perception of value. I might add that it is a short step from making sense of nonsense to making a profit on information.

Many people from all walks of life earn profits or wages by adding perceived value to what they do everyday, and usually it requires they unlock the value of information that may confuse or even overwhelm other people.

Certainly the doctors and lawyers have survived some degree of information overload in the course of their study to achieve their credentials. However, even they acknowledged the level of information coming at them is increasing and they like everyone else need some new skills and some time to get focused.

The automotive technician has always needed special tools of one kind or another, but today they need tools that give them a grip on information not just a hard to reach nut or bolt. Information affects not only the optimal operation of the engine, but virtually every system in the vehicle. When they attempt to diagnose any fault in these systems they need several types of understanding. First a complete understanding of how components are suppose to work and this includes how they send and receive information. Secondly they need expert understanding of the step by step trouble shooting process and any of the tools they will use. This might explain why attempts by

Chapter 1. Why should this stuff interest me?

less than qualified technicians provide unsatisfactory results. Their attention to what components send and receive and how it is done is increasingly important. To achieve all this understanding requires constant attention to automotive innovations and the training they need to become competent to repair new vehicles.

The school teachers acknowledge they have been under pressure to deliver students that can demonstrate measurable skills. While arguing that education is not training they have in some instances just had to deliver greater quantities of content to satisfy the political powers to be. Students like teachers have experienced information overload by mandated programs that don't seem to have much to do with traditional teaching. The frustration as a result of being overwhelmed by information is on the rise and definitely a concern of the teachers and students.

Engineers have had to use not only more technology to gain on the competition, but they have had to improve processes through the use of statistics, systems thinking and attention to customer concerns for quality. It all adds up to managing more information.

Scientists occasionally are asked, can they avoid the trap of junk science? Do they stringently apply the scientific method to their investigations, and use blind or double blind studies to support theories instead of vague unfounded references? Yes they do, but some of the less than scientific reports may be a starting point for developing a hypothesis that is then subject to greater scrutiny. Discoveries as a rule are not predictable, and a certain amount of trial

Chapter 1. Why should this stuff interest me?

and error as well as good guesswork leads to what is later recognized as a scientific discovery. How scientists use information to reach their conclusions is under constant scrutiny.

If stock brokers could make better sense of information coming at them they would be able to provide better choices for investors. There is more to brokering stock than providing the best choice for the customer, the portfolio they support may be limited by the brokerage choices available. Brokers need to do analysis of information to balance winning or losing tens of thousands of dollars in minutes not necessarily hours. Technology that may provide quick feedback is secondary to analysis of the information available that makes winners and losers.

Computer programmers admit that despite their knowledge and the numerous tools they use there are still times when they are overwhelmed by the volume of information that needs to be considered to make short and long term decisions. This work is complicated, because programs are not only used by other machines they are used by people at some level. Programs that transfer data in cyber space between machines certainly need to provide for unexpected circumstances and can be very complicated; but programs that need to interface with human beings work on very subjective kinds of criteria. These types of programs can succeed or fail based on the color schemes used on display screens. Now when I say succeed I mean it in the greatest sense of the word; the program is not only used by a single well trained manager for a large number of people, but

Chapter 1. Why should this stuff interest me?

must be seen as almost intuitive in satisfying a much larger number of people that may use it. These types of programs appear simple in their logic, but they are elegant in their design. Programming applications for people is one of the last frontiers. Here again it is not as simple as collecting all requests and all customer feedback and then satisfying the requirements with a program. There is a great deal of decision making about what feedback is useful and what is not. Using design criteria that satisfies the "lowest common denominator" in a population may bore the paying customer.

You may not hold any of the jobs previously mentioned, but you like everyone else have had to make your way in life moving from job to job. The stress of starting a new job in part has to do with those early orientations that heap a catalog of how to information on you in one day. Regardless of how elementary someone else thinks information is; it is critical that you quickly adjust and become productive.

Some of the least sophisticated jobs require some of the greatest understanding. Jobs that expect you to deal with the public cannot orient you to the many circumstances you are apt to find yourself in from day to day. Instead you will be expected to think in real time and make quick decisions that don't offend the customer everyday based on very limited information.

Why now? Well today most work is so information dependent that it requires you learn how to engage information and make it work for you. That ability is no longer optional and you know it. You need

Chapter 1. Why should this stuff interest me?

to know how to release the power and value contained in the thoughts of others and yourself to be competitive with other people. Is your situation similar to those mentioned? If the answer is yes than you need to continue reading.

Can you collaborate with others and ignore the need to manage information? I think the answer is a resounding no. Today people don't simply collaborate with people that sit next to them. Routinely collaboration for some people is done with people that live in different countries. When discussing the number of U.S. tax returns done in India, Thomas L. Friedman states in his book *The World is Flat* 2005 , "In 2004 the number (of U.S. tax returns) was 100,000. In 2005, it is expected to be 400,000." The point is that international collaboration is not something reserved for large corporations. Individuals having their income taxes prepared might want to consider that the friendly income tax preparer down the street from them has sent their information to India for consideration before placing the final numbers on their return for them to sign.

You may not always be aware that you are collaborating with people in other countries, but information more than any other commodity has found its way to other parts of the world for processing more quickly than any other commodity. The examples of this are too numerous to mention here, but include broad categories such as medical treatment, technology, transportation, entertainment, home building and furnishings, food preparation and vending. Opting out of international collaboration is not an option, because it is already a part

Chapter 1. Why should this stuff interest me?

of many products and services we all use today.

Instead of running from the challenge, learning about information management and enriching your life with it is a very practical thing to do. You can start small and realize the value on a day to day basis. If the wealth that information provides is not squandered it has a way accumulating into a large profit. Of course managing wealth will require more information that you either acquire through investigation or pay for with other profits. I like to think of it as a normal life cycle and not so much a vicious cycle, because it is not a cycle we are likely to break despite any level of difficulty we may have in stepping through it daily.

The preceding arguments for learning more about information management have revolved around being a producer. That is to say that many of your waking hours are spent working at producing some product or service that someone wants to buy based on the value you have added to it. Now consider the other side of the equation, the consumer side of your life. If you are not producing something you are most likely consuming something. It is also very possible that today anything you produce may require some consumption as a producer.

Consider the landscaper that provides a quote for a new homeowner. The services included may require expertise in several specific categories namely planning, horticulture, stonework, woodwork, irrigation, lighting and heavy equipment operation. Now it is not unheard of for one company to provide all of that expertise, but

Chapter 1. Why should this stuff interest me?

it is very unlikely. The more likely scenario is that the landscaper has expertise in one or two of the needed areas and sub-contracts the balance of the services to people that specialize in those areas. Some companies do nothing except plan and install irrigation systems. Other companies may only provide lighting installations. Therefore even if a person sees themselves as a producer, they may need to be an informed consumer to be a better producer.

The person that sees themselves as primarily a consumer may still need to consider that managing information is a very big part of being a smart consumer. Elisabeth Leamy in her book: *The Savvy Consumer* 2004 addresses "checking out a company, contracts and the cooling off rule" only to mention a few topics that require you as a consumer to take in new information and rethink your approach to consuming if you are to avoid some of the bad experiences she talks about in her book. Consuming with discretion allows you to gain greater value from every dollar you have to spend.

Although much is made of the producer and their virtuous role in society, without the consumer we would have no need for producers. Many times in the course of history a flagging economy is propped up and even sustained on the back of consumers. While business may not be reinvesting in the economy by creating new buildings or hiring new people, because of a slow or lack luster economy, the consumer is spending and carrying the burden of sustaining the economy.

William J. Byrnes in his book *Management and the Arts* 1999

Chapter 1. Why should this stuff interest me?

says, "By unique combination of historical circumstances and the existence of what is often referred to as a market-driven or consumer-driven economy, United States has created a multibillion-dollar entertainment industry that is a mix of large professional profit and many smaller professional and nonprofessional nonprofit fine art businesses. Unlike many other nations the federal government provides minimal direct support to the arts and entertainment industry in the United States." This is not the only example of how the consumer is a well respected part of the economy, but only one of many examples of how the consumer contributes on a daily basis.

As a consumer today and in the future you will be expected to review products from around the world that make it here to this marketplace. Deciding which product delivers the best value may take grappling with information constantly. The complaints consumers typically have about products center around quality and safety. Quality is something that in many ways can be detected first by visual inspection of the consumer. The quality that is a bit more challenging to review is the quality relative to safety. If a product has been painted with lead base paints it may not be detected by a visual inspection. If the product has electrical wiring that is defective, the consumer is not likely to detect the flaws until the product fails. These are not small faults in product quality and have been controlled within the country by federal, state and perhaps local regulation. Products coming to us from third world countries have not had the same level of scrutiny and need to be viewed with greater skepticism.

Chapter 1. Why should this stuff interest me?

The emergence of the big discount retailer and their impact is in great part shaped by consumers that demand a better price while still expecting higher quality and more selection. In June of 2004 Wal-Mart stores became the largest private employer in the United States, in 2005 they were employing 1.34 million people, USA Today 2006-04-11. Consumers and their ability to sift through the many producers and providers decided that the offerings at Wal-Mart met their needs best.

It would not be fair to say that Wal-Mart serves everyone although it has succeeded in many ways. Retailers that were threatened by the wide range of products and services that Wal-Mart had offered over the years have had to either add value to their offerings or lower the price. Many new small businesses have been created that do not require the bricks and mortar that a Wal-Mart store requires by locating and doing business "On the Web." Other retailers that did not want to lower their price marketed their products as premium grade. Consumers that agreed with that premise continued to buy those products at a premium price. Consumers have changed the way they review products and retailers in an information age. No longer is the consumer dependant on a newspaper ad to inform them of what is available and what has value. Consumers like producers can subcontract their search for product information, employing people that virtually work for free, by using the internet. It is not a neat and tidy process, because any search for information on the internet customarily brings back thousands of answers to a single question.

Chapter 1. Why should this stuff interest me?

How do we make sense of it all? How does the consumer improve their search for products, services and information? Part of the answer is preparation.

So if you are a producer or a consumer your need to process information is a never ending and ever expanding task that will be improved by learning to better process information. Regardless of anything you have learned before there is always more to learn that may enhance your experience as a consumer or as a producer. So if you are ready to prepare yourself for a better experience than you have had in the past you need to continue reading.

Learning new skills and an improved process is important, but you may find what you learn about yourself more significant. Self examination will enable you to be a leader not a follower. Following a leader is only a disadvantage if you have no capacity to lead yourself. As a leader you will be better able share decision making or standing in for an absent leader. Knowing yourself can improve the way you approach any task or the preparation that is always needed.

Preparing starts with developing a mindset including a set of tools and techniques. These are not just pieces of technology that you will buy at the nearest electronics store. This is, for the most part, thinking that everyone has access to, but not all people choose to consider. This approach is intuitive, because it is used routinely when most of us are not making a conscious choice to do things differently. Similar tools and techniques for handling information in dissimilar situations are used by people that have nothing in common with you

Chapter 1. Why should this stuff interest me?

other than perhaps their need to manage information.

CHAPTER 2

Preparing to Process Information

Just as preparing a room to paint is important to the painting process so is the preparation for processing information to the actual act of processing information. Developing a mindset that guides you as an individual and helps focus your actions in a way that enhances your ability to use information is critical. Once you have established a mindset you can consider what tools are available for managing the information you will encounter.

Ascribe value to those items that make a difference in your life today, tomorrow and in a future you can visualize. This is similar to the concept of a developing a "value mindset" spelled out in *The Value Mindset* by Eric Stern and Mike Hutchinson 2004. The author's state, "The value mindset is a revolutionary concept, in that it returns to the very roots of capitalism: the concept of investing resources in order to generate a return based on risk taken." Would you extend yourself to collect, analyze and use information that had no potential to provide some return beyond the time and effort it took to collect it?

Chapter 2. Preparing to Process Information

Hopefully your answer to that question would be a resounding no. Connect yourself to information that has personal value. Information presented to you usually is structured in a way that tries to connect with you, so having established specific values prepares you for any encounter. How is a mindset organized on a moments notice?

Start with the topic. No matter what the circumstance, a casual conversation, a business meeting or a formal presentation. Meetings provide an opportunity to collect valuable information. These situations all revolve around topics that can be used to generate questions and offer opportunities to put forth your ideas for consideration and feedback.

Prioritizing the topics of information that most interest you can also alert you to opportunities for engaging someone in conversation. At the top of your list will probably be topics that directly impact the health or wealth of yourself or someone close to you. These are the topics that you are most likely to feel passionately about on almost any day. When you identify a topic of interest within a conversation, engage the person with questions that you may have accumulated. Business or investment priorities are almost always included within those topics unless you perhaps live very modestly on a fixed income. Even then there may be some interest in what it takes to keep what you have established. We need to understand how our welfare is directly connected to our priority list of the subjects we are interested in addressing in conversation. Human nature will guide you even when you deny an interest in most things. Knowing that creates an opportunity to focus on business and determine which priorities can advance your business interest and welfare. Those topics are topics we can be passionate about and gain the most by discussing with others. We discuss these topics in an effort to unlock the value of information that others have a key to, and are ready to share.

If you seek understanding of a topic don't assume someone is going to bring the information to you. Seeking out people with special understanding needs to be a part of your everyday life. There are many ways to communicate with people today given technology, but that only establishes the connection. Relationships that provide insight and knowledge are developed over time through dialogue and interaction with knowledgeable people. Learn to enjoy the search for those people that can inform you and guide you toward greater understanding. The journey is a learning experience onto itself that is different for each person. As you establish a relationship with a person get to know them and their passions.

Get to know the strengths of the person you are engaging in a conversation. If the person is skilled or knowledgeable in preparing food your questions about dressmaking may be misplaced. If the person has made a business of food preparation business questions are appropriate even if the best they can do is give you a referral. The strengths of other people in the conversation will add depth and passion to the answers they provide on relevant questions. Questions that focus on the passions of others usually provide thoughtful answers that will tend to have greater value. Try to narrow your focus. If all you expect are general answers you degrade the value of the answer before it is given.

Sharing what you know with others while learning new and interesting information from them establishes a network that can be a very valuable. Most accomplished people will be quick to credit the effort others have contributed to their personal success that may have been sudden or long in coming. I suppose the less ambitious you are the less important a network would seem. However, networks can be supportive of some of the seemingly least ambitious goals. For example if the only goal you had was to have a long healthy life a network of health care professionals that consult you on both staying healthy and overcoming illness could be critical. Don't be quick to discount the value of information other people may contribute to your achieving goals in life no matter how simple they may seem.

Every encounter presents opportunity to learn, review or sound out information. This does not mean that all encounters need to be scrutinized, but as you learn to establish a mindset and use some of the following tools it will be difficult to engage others without establishing a meaningful connection. When I think of tools my first thought is not a gadget. Tools are those inanimate things that every person has "onboard" and may choose to use or not use. That means you don't need to go to the electronics store to get equipped, you already are fully equipped. Any gadgetry you purchase is optional. As you review these "tools" ask yourself, is this something I am prepared to use?

Chapter 2. Preparing to Process Information

The Question is the first "Tool" in your toolbox. It can be used in many circumstances making it very powerful. When things are moving to fast for you, the easiest way to slow the rate of incoming information is to ask questions. A question requires the presenter to think. Will they simply repeat the previously made point or will they opt to rephrase their point? Either way the presentation is slowed. A question also helps make information relevant; it helps personalize information making it much easier to remember.

What about information dumping that people encounter in job orientation or training, a departmental meeting, a managers meeting, a seminar, a convention meeting, an association meeting, etc. Should we be addressing the root cause of why this happens or how to deal with it in real time? The answer is, just learn to engage it and deal with it in real time. One easy way to do this in a job orientation is to ask to do the job while the trainer observes and guides your direction. It simply puts the burden on the presenter to observe how you use the information you have been given. Initially it might seem more stressful, but it gives you time to practice what you are expected to learn. Meetings and seminars may require a different approach.

Let's have some fun with this by applying some imagination. We will place you somewhere in the future to illustrate my point. Given the importance and value of information, in the future specialists will be available to deal with overwhelming volumes of information that companies and organizations compile for one day seminars. You will be the information specialist. Now let's visit

Chapter 2. Preparing to Process Information

some time and place in the future.

Imagine yourself an Emergency Information Technician (EIT), and you have just been called to an Information Dumping. It is rather important information, but between the light show, the cartoon graphics the music and the dialogue of the speaker few people are apt to remember much of anything. You can help some members of the audience if only you can stop the hemorrhaging of information, so just as any good Emergency Medical Technician (EMT) the EIT needs to focus on life saving priorities. Like a Samurai with the skill of a thousand years you interrupt with a pointed question that strikes right to the heart of the speaker and he can't resist a pause that gives others time to shake off that "Deer in the Headlights Stare". Once the presentation opens up to questions be sure to have enough to stop them cold in their tracks. Just as an EMT applies pressure to an open wound, to stop the bleeding, so to the EIT can shut off a flood of information with the pressure of questioning. Asking for relevant examples of what is explained or simply a rephrasing of some point that is important. Eventually they will call time and the emergency will be under control and an entire audience is spared a fate worse than death, "Information Overload". The key here is preparation in advance.

Most people go to one day seminars unprepared to ask questions. Doing research ahead of any seminar gives you an edge when topics advertised are addressed. Your questions fill in the "pot holes" that provide a connection from general information to applied learning. Instead of only taking back information that could have been extracted from a book, you take back a new opinion on how this new information can make a difference in your work environment.

Catalog and store the valued information in categories that make sense to you. Using generic file systems make retrieval of information slow. Relational databases have been around for some time now. This type of database either electronic or manual paper files have made it easy to slice and dice information many ways. Remember, if you haven't established what information is needed ahead of attending a conference the chance of you collecting what is needed once you get there is not very good. Become a diligent customer; identify the nature of the event and the relevant value of information you need to retrieve for your business.

Your work isn't done however until you transport the information safely back to a place where it can be properly managed, so compare and rewrite notes soon after the meeting to make them as complete as possible. Check for handout copies of the slides. Positioning yourself or someone else near the speaker or an apparent supply of handout material that will be distributed at the end of the presentation is a smart move. If recording is permitted, record and review. If you have a note pad, use it. If others in your team are able to assist, ask them to help. Don't waste any time transporting information back to the office, seconds count. Do it electronically if possible and your mission is complete.

Stepping back from our imaginary example, how can we

Chapter 2. Preparing to Process Information

get the most from a business meeting? Analysis can start with the agenda. The people that organize and conduct the meetings usually have an agenda that isn't subject to much change. You are there to collect information first and foremost, and then analyze it at a rate that gives us time to put things into a proper perspective and finally store it in a way that allows easy access in the future. Some analysis is done during collection, but you may want other collaborators to raise questions. What is missing? Good analysis will require energy.

Energy is developed when asking questions between the speakers and the audience; this is not a regular occurrence, because we are limited by rules the speaker imposes on the audience, but this energy helps analyze the information and helps determine what is worth attaching to our current base of information.

Motivational speakers conduct seminars that purposely generate participant enthusiasm. The difference is they organize it and conduct meetings in a way that promotes an exchange of information unlike so many other everyday meetings that do not aim to be energetic. Motivational speakers realize their message is far more likely to have a lasting affect if they connect with the audience, and they work to achieve this affect. The speaker makes the rules, but it is not impossible to be the spark that starts a fire under everyone as a participant. Usually speakers welcome enthusiastic participants that stay on topic.

Let's discuss a second tool you can carry and have available at all times. **The Picture** or the ability to visualize. It is even more powerful, because it serves several purposes. Like the question it can help you connect new information with information already known, but more than that it allows you to construct a virtual reality not otherwise available.

Some people may possess a greater aptitude for visualization than others, but all people have an inherent talent latent within them. If you doubt me read this list of words to yourself and see if they generate a picture, or only register as words on paper with written definitions:

Elephant

Dog

Bed

Certainly the pictures people generate will vary, but the images these words and others generate are significant. As you read those words could you prevent an image from forming ? My guess is your answer is NO! Once again this demonstrates the power of pictures.

To use this ability as a tool on information takes a bit of practice, but the benefits are worth your time. First focus on the images that occur to you as a result of all your sensory input and secondly link it to known information. You know you are doing it right if your images are striking, have meaning, and are easy to recall. People famous for demonstrating their ability to remember have fostered this approach to improving memory for many years. Harry Lorayne and Jerry Lucas in *The Memory Book: The Classic Guide to Improving Your Memory at Work, at School, and at Play*

Chapter 2. Preparing to Process Information

2000 talk about their method that can enhance your memory through practice using a process for associating striking images with information. Improved recall based on your stored images can and will improve how you deal with floods of information. Try to find simple ways to practice this daily.

Well we have briefly scratched the surface of what you need to do when you are faced with a situation that may provide more information than you are prepared to handle comfortably. Let us visit another imaginary meeting room where information will be delivered at the speed of light. Will you begin to approach it as I might? It is not enough to clean and polish your tools; you must learn to use your tools in situations that connect your survival to using information, if you are to be prepared for the real world. Are you ready?

Let me set the scene, some of you might be already familiar with it. Your company has sent you to a convention and asked you to attend the meetings that will help them make a decision on the next generation of copy machine they need to consider. The company you work for is medium size with several thousand employees at several locations. We are at a large convention hall, and literally hundreds of people are milling around rather casually. Some guests simply identify people in their party and sit down next to them with no concern for the event about to be held. Now people select certain seats for very specific reasons. Some of those reasons have nothing to do with gathering information or participating in discussion from the floor. Given the situation I describe, where should we sit?

Chapter 2. Preparing to Process Information

We should look for seats that first give the best view of the speaker and any presentation they might have planned. Sometimes a podium and a large projection screen are obvious. We may need seats near any floor microphone if we hope to participate, and we should scout out any handout materials that may be available. Handouts can be particularly helpful in identifying key elements of the presentation worth questioning. Handouts can also help generate discussion around topics that match your mindset values. Consider the perspective of the speaker ahead of the presentation to prepare you for questions.

Consider, you need to approach this get together with a mission in mind. That is just how you need to think to stay focused. The old axiom about "only getting out of something what you put into it" will definitely hold true here. If you are attending with a real purpose in mind you are far more likely to take a closer look at everything that transpires. A team approach is more effective in this situation than working it alone.

Would it have helped if we had brainstormed some of the methods or technology that could back us up before meeting at the conference? Yes, I started your scenario somewhat after that opportunity, but only to emphasize how those kinds of thoughts will pop into your mind a day late. Deliberation ahead of time on agendas and the purpose for attending the meeting will provide preparation that cannot be done out of sequence.

I will stop to mention that we have discovered the third tool out of sheer need, **The Thought**. Assessing the situation described

Chapter 2. Preparing to Process Information

requires the thought, what needs to be done? You used your ability to think and identified what was needed to accomplish your mission. Thinking has its place and usually that is early and frequently. The later you wait to get engaged mentally the faster you will be obliged to think as time passes.

Here is a clear example of how that comes into play. A skydiver, a person that jumps out of planes and parachutes to the ground after some time spent in freefall, has an endless amount of time to pack their parachute properly, but if they were distracted and skip a crucial step or made an error the next opportunity to review that process or take corrective action would be during freefall. When the skydiver pulls their rip cord to deploy their parachute the time left for decision making customarily may be down to about 10 seconds. Minutes of focused preparation ahead of time would seem to be a small price to pay to avoid last minute emergency procedures.

Next consider **The Act**. It will compete with thinking, because knowing what to do to survive will never replace doing what it takes to survive. Your ability to question, picture, think and analyze will help, but you must act!

By now I think your beginning to realize that preparing to process information may require technology, but the tools that will distinguish you from the crowd are **Fundamental Thought Processes**. We all have different capacities to think clearly and efficiently when it comes to gathering and processing information. Mikel Harry and Richard Schroeder, have done some extensive work on achieving quality and efficiency by scrutinizing processes in their book *Six Sigma, The Breakthrough Management Strategy Revolutionizing The World's Top Corporations 2006*. Our approach to process use and improvement is dwarfed by their effort, but we can take a simple lesson from their work. Mikel Harry and Richard Schroeder say, "Six Sigma represents extraordinary sense, not ordinary or common sense; common sense rarely produces extraordinary results." I would conclude the real advantage of focusing on the processes that lead to results is that it tends to lead to process improvement and measurable quality improvement.

Just using some simple and effective approaches you can demonstrate abilities you only wished you had before now. This will move you gently and swiftly into the twenty-first century where managing information well is a necessary part of jobs that pay well.

If thought processes are fundamental then methods or techniques for increasing the speed of these processes would seem helpful. Actually most people have structured their work in a way that keeps their brain processing information at an efficient and an accustomed speed. Your brain normally is taking in information from all senses and prioritizing the most important information first. For example you may be focused on following the instructions for a favorite recipe and while going through the motions of cooking all of a sudden you burn yourself on the stove. Certainly your body knows enough to interrupt everything else and recoil from the source of the pain you experience without you taking time to decide is this pain important? This kind of thinking and information processing I refer to as **Parallel Processing**.

Busy people routinely use their natural ability to do this. If however you don't discipline yourself to manage multiple tasks this natural advantage is lost. A way to take advantage of this is to arrange your work so that many things can happen at once, giving your attention only to what is needed to maintain the process and acceptable outcomes. A Juggler that keeps many plates spinning is a simple and vivid example of how this works. How many times have you referred to how you manage your work as "Juggling" your work load? Unfortunately many people perceive juggling work task assignments as something to be avoided. As for me it is only another way to shorten the distance between start and finish. Even if you can't change the time from start of a task to finish, consider how long the work has been in the queue since it was assigned? That is the measure the rest of the world is familiar with and uses to grade performance.

When industries in this country have a backlog of work other countries look at that as an opportunity to shorten the queue time for customers that don't want to wait. How can information be processed in parallel? How can you process more information in less time. Without getting into a dissertation on computer chips, think about information handling that needs your attention only some of the time not all of the time. This is an opportunity to combine a variety of information management tasks into a parallel process. You will complete many more tasks when you process them all at the same time than if you line them up one after the other in series.

If you still need some real world examples of this let me name a few. Walking around on two legs, beyond requiring a physical capacity requires you respond to information relayed to you through your senses in parallel. If you don't agree put on a blindfold and note your caution when you attempt to walk. Think back to a time when one of your limbs went numb, because of an awkward sitting position. If you stood to walk at that moment to relieve the numbness things may not have gone exactly as you had expected. When the telephone rings what happens? A careful review will demonstrate you process information in parallel even if it initially might seem to be a series of tasks. These should give you an idea of how natural parallel processing is when you aren't giving it consideration.

Consider that some of the stress you currently experience, when it comes to information handling, is due to doing most things in series and avoiding a more natural parallel process. Using queues can provide opportunities to parallel process under peak load times if additional resources are available. Queues also can allow batching work using limited resources.

In my last position with General Motors I prepared paperwork in a procurement process that while not perfect did provide queues to manage workflow. The individual tasks were serial like, because each contract was separately processed, although queuing work provided opportunities to do steps in parallel. Each type of work had a different set of steps to completion with events in each process that might

Chapter 2. Preparing to Process Information

require waiting time for signatures. At that point all contracts were similar in as much as they all were waiting for the same consideration and set of signatures. All work that had to wait took a place in queue.

During some periods I might have as many as 15-20 jobs waiting for feedback or information from someone in the process. That was not difficult to keep track of even with a combination of paper and electronic files. The queue was the place in the process that allowed intermittent work for jobs that had incomplete information. Multiple people could work from the queue on high volume days in parallel. Queues also allowed batching of contracts. If five contracts were waiting for signatures all five would be done at the first opportunity.

Like the juggler I would work on jobs from the queue that had sufficient information alternately adding information from the confirming telephone call, the requested estimate, the signature, etc., etc. methodically and without delays moving from one task to another. The only difficulty was trying to shorten the wasted wait time that we had no direct control over. We could influence remaining time by escalating the issue, but that was like pulling the fire alarm two or three times a day. At some point it would become clear that the fire drills were compromising the larger system. From the customers perspective the wait time was excessive without good reason. From the individuals perspective inside the process too many requests were marked urgent.

When I retired the transition was simple. All I needed to do was pick up my queue of file folders that were waiting and place them onto the desk of my partner that did similar work. I no longer had to wait for anything, but it instantly doubled the work in the waiting queue on my teammates' desk.

The advantage to the larger process was the waiting was done in parallel allowing one person to process an increased workload, or any number of people to share the workload by pulling work from the queue. Queuing work allows for overflow and multiple people doing work from the same queue in parallel. The process had positive and negative attributes, but that was a significant improvement over old methods.

Regardless of serial or parallel processes when the objective is to collect, analyze and store information analysis is the key, because it is needed throughout the process. Analysis helps us determine the information worthy of collection in at least two ways. First it helps determine usefulness relative to some priority list of topics or a specific mindset. Second we determine useful attributes that can later be used to link or store information for relational reporting.

Are there any links associated with the person or place that is the source of the information you found? There will be times when you will want to go back and ask another question, links to the source of information don't leave you saying: "Where did that information come from?" Even if the links are an informal reference they will give you a clue or a starting point.

Here again you need to think ahead of your pursuit of

Chapter 2. Preparing to Process Information

information. Thinking ahead of an event boils down to preparation. Preparing to manage information will always make you better able to collect and store the information with proper reference.

Preparing yourself should include an honest assessment of your approach to processing information. It is difficult to do this yourself, but some assessment is better than none. You could employ a third party that would be more objective instead of a do-it-yourself approach. The assessment will tend to put you in touch with your individual traits. Knowing what to do and what tools work for you will help, but getting things done can take many routes. Understanding your style and approach to being successful will support the patience you will need to sustain extended efforts. Self assessment will need to eventually happen if you are to become a self-starter.

A self assessment does not need to be a self inflicted flogging. Keep it positive, so what is determined can make a positive difference. Consider the positive ways you have overcome adversity in the past. Even if you consider yourself unsuccessful overall stop and look deeper for small moments of success. Less important events that have positive outcomes need to be used by you as a model for success in the future. These instances are your experience and are the basis for a much greater success in the future.

Identify specific behaviors you use to turn a negative situation positive. Here are some possible answers that might fit your personality.

Chapter 2. Preparing to Process Information

- Get quiet when trying to focus on what needs to be done.

- Get energy by doing simple tasks first.

- Rely on regular breaks to manage stress

- Rely on a structured environment to make progress.

- Depend on a diversity of tasks to stay energized.

Find your own list of positive enablers that fit you. Make the list as long as you can without repeating yourself.

Knowing what makes you successful can be more valuable than a suitcase full of expensive tools. Learning from yourself those things that make you successful will make you a self-starter everywhere you go. Do not minimize the impact it will have on how others look at you or more importantly how you look at yourself.

While stepping into a role unfamiliar to me I learned first hand how important the previously mentioned tools kept the experience from being overwhelming. I went from novice instructor to grizzled instructor in the period of one year. The first step for me was establishing a mindset that would carry me through what would be a rather challenging year. I had already established some rudimentary skills as an instructor/mentor, so I dispensed with a further assessment.

I was working as a contracting designer when this opportunity came up and that made it easy to transition from my normal contracting activities to this position as an instructor. I could still do some limited contracting while I worked at a technical institute. I had mentored young designers as part of an ordinary daily routine and instructing them in a more formal setting did not appear to be

Chapter 2. Preparing to Process Information

significantly different. I was wrong, but more about that later.

In the most general way I was determined to initially get familiar with the existing curriculum and organize the students into project teams that would develop personal portfolios that could be used for job interviews. To my dismay the curriculum was not sufficient to lead these young people into the work world. This put me at odds with the management that did not agree. I was determined to change the direction on the current program regardless. These students were in twelve month and eighteen month programs that were expected to make them ready for jobs at an entry level. These were all post high school students that had jobs and little time for homework.

My first day as an instructor was chaotic and somewhat unexpected. Many students seemed rather hostile and others were just complacent. As I began to ask questions and listen to the students some rather interesting facts bubbled to the surface.

The two previous instructors had come to class intoxicated and they assumed I was about to be the third such instructor. The program they were following did not seem to have much relevance to the jobs they were interested in having after their schooling. It seemed clear to me that these students needed a perspective that reassured them that they were developing skills they could use to make them productive.

Those early days were critical to students developing a mindset that could guide these twenty students through a learning experience. I needed to share my view of the world with them, so they could be enthusiastic about what they needed to do every day they came to school. One way I did that was by introducing them to other people in the workplaces they hoped to be in twelve months or eighteen months from that time. We took a field trip to an architectural firm for those students that would develop heating and cooling systems for the buildings. We took a field trip to the Detroit News for illustrators that would be developing illustration portfolios related to advertising. Design students that would develop tool design portfolios visited the Ford Motor Company. After only a month or so the classroom was busy developing portfolios for their perspective employers. The previous books used became useful references, but were not what shaped the student mindset.

These students were focused on developing references that would be their calling card anywhere they applied for a job. My role became one of a coach. I would answer questions and question their decisions guiding them through new experiences. Many times it was like juggling twenty plates without letting one fall to the floor. The student needed to think about the project they decided to embark on, was it one that would get the attention of a perspective employer? Did the project demonstrate their skills? What were employers looking for in their new employees? Was the quality of the students work comparable to what they had seen on the field trips they took?

The students became engaged and took responsibility for work that would make them successful. They became their own best advocates, asking questions and thinking for themselves with that mindset or vision of what needed to be accomplished. I needed to do a

Chapter 2. Preparing to Process Information

bit of parallel processing, because as time went on the classes grew from having twenty or so students to as many as forty five or so at any given time. Some of the students were from previous classes that just wanted to work on their project between classes, but others were new with individual needs. The questions students had span nine distinct categories requiring analysis and questioning of each student.

Needless to say the daily routine was challenging, but after six months the environment was as originally envisioned and to the relief of many students. At the end of that year the students, at the request of a local engineering company, made one last field trip to introduce them to a potential employer. A company representative reviewed student portfolios and offered many entry positions that day. Other students had already secured positions ahead of their graduation and some had become free lance designers and illustrators.

As for me I went back to a much less rigorous and more comfortable contracting design business. I was wiser and richer from the experience that others contributed to every day.

CHAPTER 3

Engaging the Other Person

When you engage someone in conversation collecting everything they have to say is not the answer. As Norbert Weiner said in his book The *Human Use of Human Beings* 1969 "Speech is a joint game between the talker and the listener against the force of confusion. Unless both make the effort, interpersonal communication is quite hopeless." To make decisions on what to collect for further consideration we need to consider collecting what is observable, measurable and of value. This alone will help you cut the task of collecting at least fifty percent. Recognize your time is important and seek to limit the time spent collecting information. Let me help you identify some steps you can take to improve your collection process.

The following questions that need to be asked are important to establishing a mindset that identifies the value further discussion will reinforce. Values are the "glue" that hold together and support some purpose for any discussion you may have with regard to any given

Chapter 3. Engaging the Other Person

topic. Knowing yourself and what you value makes all real-time processing and sorting easy, because it helps you raise appropriate questions in a timely way. Not having a well defined set of values to bounce all ideas off of leaves you with an enormous amount of information that may or may not have value being collected and unquestioned. Although establishing core values is well beyond the scope of this book, a way to establish some basic well defined rules that drive managing information today is to ask some simple questions ahead of any meeting.

Is your inquiry driven by a clear and easily described purpose that establishes the value of your effort? If you cannot describe your purpose for questioning others in a few words, they may lack interest in answering your inquiry. Even if you pay a person to discuss a topic there should be a clear purpose they are there to satisfy. Without a clear purpose answers may be generated that have wide application and serve no single purpose. How does the purpose of your inquiry impact you? If the purpose is a low priority or less important in nature it will be communicated in your questioning. You probably would not communicate any sense of urgency around getting accurate specific answers to your questions.

Who will you meet with to exchange information? If the person is familiar to you or has a close relationship with you, the engagement will include more opportunity for subjective measurement as compared to strangers who are more easily measured by objective means. Be prepared with written objectives and questions ahead of a meeting, it helps make any meeting objective with measurable results.

What will the agenda address? An agreed to agenda helps you keep discussions on track and permits you to quickly discount information outside the agenda topics. An agenda allows for preparation in advance of any meeting where information is exchanged and evaluated.

When will you meet? Is there any appointment or will it be an impromptu meeting at a time and place uncertain. Identifying a time and place adds certainty to a meeting and generally will facilitate other things that need to happen before and after the meeting.

Where will you meet? Is transportation required? What is the backup plan? Maybe a telephone conversation can be an alternative to a personal meeting if schedules are tight. Sometimes locations can make the meeting more congenial than it might have been otherwise. How will where you meet impact the meeting?

What are the next steps after the meeting? Did the meeting resolve some problem or answer questions that needed answers, or was the intention just to move a dialogue forward to a different level of understanding?

Let's look at an example where it is very difficult to control objectivity. Some of the best examples involve people with whom we have established relationships. In these instances we tend to act emotional rather than rational and put ourselves at a disadvantage when it comes to collecting needed information.

If a loved one is saying something, regardless of its

Chapter 3. Engaging the Other Person

significance to the state of the world, the cost of tea in China, or even its impact on tax credits, you may ignore any part of what is being said only at your own risk. Ignoring what is said will be perceived as rude and is apt to spawn what might seem to be a senseless argument. Managing the extra information in a cordial and loving way is more likely to leave time for more conversations that may be more meaningful to you. This is an example that requires very careful consideration of what information is to be discarded. Even though I still don't encourage collecting everything, this situation may require a very careful sorting process. Stretching the criteria that identifies what is important is appropriate here. Try to get a sense of the issues that need to be addressed as a first step in a longer process of dialogue with loved ones.

Use your senses to identify what is observable and use your mind to determine what is measurable and of value. What is the general appearance of the person? Does this tell you something about the content of what is being said? What is being emphasized? Is it clearly defined or referred to without being said? Besides physical appearances, does the person seem emotional about the subject? Regardless of first appearances try to provide time to listen before responding. These kinds of situations are probably the most dynamic, and you need to remember you collect information with your eyes and your ears not with your mouth.

Controlling these situations isn't near as important as determining where do you go from here. If you have done a good job of collecting information as discussed, and you have verified it by putting it in your own words to get verification, take the next step. Suggest some time to think about what was said to provide either a measured response or a graceful exit.

There are a number of steps you can take from the start of a conversation to the end. To decide early what is important to remember or to collect; ask yourself why is this conversation taking place? Is it for the purpose of vocalizing what up to now has been just thought about and not expressed? Is it to help rationalize what seems irrational? Is it to ask for help? Whatever the answer is don't hesitate to consider the question of why first and then confirm the answer with others to insure your perspective isn't too narrow.

Another question to ask, when you want to narrow things down, is what is the topic? How many times have you had a conversation that seems to ramble and leaves you confused? You might hear yourself say, what was all of that about? To find out what the conversation is about ask questions. You might be surprised at the answers, but you will better understand the topic of your conversation.

Now ask, when and what is supposed to happen as of a result of this conversation? If you haven't heard a time mentioned ask about one. Today, tomorrow, a week from today, a year from today, some undetermined date in the future? Any one of those answers may be valid answers to the question, but they are different and not understood unless either asked or offered directly.

Where will things occur? Specifically what location, your

Chapter 3. Engaging the Other Person

house or mine, the bank or the cafe, here or someplace yet to be determined? All possible, but not understood unless confirmed. Ask, who needs to take action? It needs to be answered as do all the other questions, because these answers help limit that elastic criteria that helps determine what to collect.

Sometimes we avoid asking the questions, because we don't want to hear the answers. Who ever thought that collecting information took courage? Well surprise, collecting information may be a more noble adventure than any of us first thought; you may even find it exciting at some point, but more about that later. Meanwhile, make asking questions for the purpose of gathering information a mandatory requirement any time you engage a person or a group in conversation.

At the other end of the spectrum we consider a discussion in a business environment. If the meeting starts without an agenda, or at least without one that is published there may be an elastic collection criteria. Hidden agendas always exist and may get people rambling. If it is a situation that requires a facilitator, the facilitator should not allow people to get off track for extended periods of time introducing issues that go beyond the scope of the meeting. If this happens you may suggest that some issues be recorded and set aside for discussion at another time. Our own notes can legitimately discard anecdotes, but what about the politics? As Andrew J. Dubrins said in his book *Winning Office Politics* 1990, "Politics are played to obtain power-the ability to control people or resources, or to get others to do things you want done." Remember, we are still dealing with thoughts generated by a person that may need or just want consideration. There may not be incentive to collect these remarks verbatim, but they may reveal a familiar agenda worth noting. Generally, business objectives are the key to sorting anecdotes from the rest of the conversation. When you prepare for a business meeting review the agenda to determine what information you may need to probe for or what information you may be expected to provide for others. These criteria can be controlled and far less elastic.

You can see how quickly we get mired down in an endless collecting process especially if we have not given the process some thought up front. That brings us to that "scientific method" mentioned earlier. This generally implies being determined to collect what is observable and measurable. Not an easy task when it comes to words that may have several meanings when considered by several people. To be quick about it you must record your impression and in summary form whenever possible. Collect dates, names, important points and your first impressions. You can always compare your notes later with a colleague to review your impression of the remarks made, but without your first impression of the remark it may not even get consideration.

Next sort what information is of value. Do your best to sort it as you hear it, see it, or simply as you become aware of it. This needs to be realized early to avoid cluttering your schedule with offline sorting. Always be sensitive to the impact information management

Chapter 3. Engaging the Other Person

may have on other objectives you need to address. The scientific process of collecting information should help you collect data associated with what is said and done in a brief format.

Did you actually see it, or hear it and did you put it in a context that reflected the presenter of the information. So many times in our collection of information we contaminate the information with our own interpretations. We do it without thinking. What we need to do is to think in a conscious way to improve the quality of our information collection. Otherwise we are subject to that old axiom with an unknown author, "Garbage in Garbage out." In other words if the information we collect isn't free of our own bias we may report impressions that don't reflect the presentation.

Your role is important to the collection process, because it defines the scope of your involvement and your interest in information available. Do you have ownership? Are you a liaison between interested parties? Are you a consultant or key decision maker or are you someone who has the task of doing the tasks whatever they may be? Let's look at how your role may change the way you collect information.

If you have ownership, the kind of ownership that affects your fortunes directly, your level of interest in all information is generally more intense on all fronts. The ownership can be literal or implied, but unless you assume ownership your behavior is not likely to reflect any intensity. Conduct the following simple experiment that will demonstrate this point. Think of something for which you have no

Chapter 3. Engaging the Other Person

ownership an object, or a process. Objects could include a vehicle, a child, a pet, etc.. Processes might include a recipe, or a method for doing some work task, etc.. Visualize it clearly enough to be able to describe it to someone else. Now take ownership by imagining a real connection between yourself and it. Remember the connection must be significant. You are the expert when it comes to the object or process of your choice. As you establish a connection even though only in your mind for this moment you should begin to experience a higher awareness of the situation you have described to yourself. If you catch yourself considering the impact on your life great and small previously not considered you have officially taken ownership. It should demonstrate how your interest improved when ownership is established, and perhaps how your view of things changed.

The real lesson to be learned regarding your role when collecting information is, take ownership if only in your own mind. Your improved awareness will have you asking all the right questions and controlling the flow of information. Your interest and enthusiasm will make the effort painless and efficient.

OK, let's review. Collecting information does not mean collecting everything. When you collect you need a strategy, some specific questions, a "scientific method", that helps you separate what you need from everything else, and do it in "real time" or as it happens to the extent you can. Sorting through information as it is shared frees up time after for real analysis of the information. Perhaps additional time may be used to test any conclusions that are drawn from your

Chapter 3. Engaging the Other Person

information collection and analysis. Robert Todd Carroll, author of: "*The Skeptics Dictionary*" 2007, clearly explains at his web site, http://skepdic.com/control.html, how control groups and double blind tests can help separate fact from fiction. Bolstering arguments with testing that is repeatable is likely to give your argument greater credibility.

You most likely will need to ask questions in almost every instance, because when people present ideas they can't hear or see what is presented from your perspective. That is why they invite questions either directly or indirectly. The questions you need to ask are why?, what?, when?, where?, and who? After, you repeat the answers back in your own words and get confirmation that you properly understand what was said; you have a good basis for thinking more deeply. Don't forget how your role can impact your interest in what is presented. If you perceive yourself as an owner it raises your sense of interest in all information and is likely to have you asking questions that will get to the information you need.

One of your first objectives should be to collect information about people, because they will be an extended resource of information. How valuable is their perspective to a discussion? Other natural owners such as managers may have control over tasks that need to occur, so beyond your collection do not underestimate the value others have relative to information collection. Get past the notion that you and you alone hold all necessary facts. Consider the objective and subjective collections of others. The collective understanding of others is likely to provide answers to questions that go beyond your own experience.

What we need now are a few examples that can help illustrate what we have been talking about, but rather than tell tales from long ago I think it would be instructive to construct some probable situations. As you read, certain questions should come to mind.

Our first situation could be described as a calamity if the demeanor of the manager is any measure of the situation. The manager of the department demands that facts concerning the current budget be gathered and reported by the close of business. Several problems exist, islands of information, no process in place that links the information, and finally no one person that knows where the most reliable information resides.

Try to start with observable and measurable information that you obtain in the original assignment. Certainly it helps if you can get permission to go to the source of the request to resolve new issues. If that isn't allowed let the person assigning the work understand that you need to regard them as the owner and content expert to expedite their request. Were fundamental questions answered when the work was assigned? What is the final format of the report? You need to identify where you are going before you proceed toward some unknown end by just doing what seems obvious, because most managers are quick to answer questions about the direction early not six hours into an eight hour project. The process of gathering and processing information to some final reporting event is one that tends

Chapter 3. Engaging the Other Person

to start slow and gather speed along the way. Are there preferred sources of information or are you allowed to reconcile what you identify as most reliable information? What preference is there to the process you follow? When must the report be delivered? All these questions precede information collection.

Now let's try to use some of the tools we discussed earlier in an effort to make practical use of what might have seemed like theoretical chatter. Where is the most reliable information? If it is a part of someone's notes, get the notes. Is it part of another report, get the report. Identify the elements you need and where they reside. Review the familiar list of sources for valid information and have someone help make the contacts that lead to a complete collection of the information. Next identify the process you are about to use to assemble the data when it arrives, and the resources necessary for this process. As things begin to happen and pieces of the puzzle are found do your best to negotiate the format the final report will take with the person making the original request if that is permitted.

Questioning is most appropriate in the early stages, but once you have distilled a direction you need to get it done. You certainly need to keep thinking as you move through the process, evaluating the product being produced as it comes together. Quality control is not the last step of a process, but instead quality control is an integral part of the process from start to finish. The manager has stated that the report needs to be complete by the close of business. If the timeline is getting tight think of ways that you can do things simultaneously and parallel process. Parallel processing can help shorten the time overall while allowing added time for added tasks.

Have you maintained your focus? Think the process through again as you move to the conclusion. It is much easier to squeeze in another consideration early in the process. Are there benchmarks that can be used to identify where you are in the process? Don't rule out being asked to report your status on an hourly basis. Part of what you may need to report is the plan you are using to get from start to finish. This is not unusual if the manager is unfamiliar with your methods and needs a reason to have confidence in your approach to what they may consider a critical mission. Finally before submitting the report, review it to match up initial requirements with the final product to avoid an embarrassing glaring error.

Even if you hadn't considered your new tools before you will only neglect them at your own expense in the future. The crisis is a common occurrence in all environments and although we all plan to avoid a crisis they happen. If we can't avoid them totally then we must survive them as gracefully and as efficiently as possible.

The second situation we need to consider is an assignment to clean clear and organize the office files. This situation needs both consideration of management and users of the files. Legislation regarding financial responsibility has made all file management important to the manager. Management must give legal consideration to files that must be retained, while users can determine the most efficient method to organize files to improve access and general use.

Chapter 3. Engaging the Other Person

Perhaps malaise, complacency, or just plain neglect has created the need for this work to be considered, but careful consideration going forward will insure a more efficient and responsive organization that is meeting it's legal obligations. Files both electronic and paper have created a virtual jungle of data. Every task, every initiative bumps up against this monster. Some people contribute to the problem as if it were a requirement of their daily assignment. It has created grid lock in several instances and only seems to serve to slow all work.

How do we apply our new tools to make things better? Although this problem seems mundane and of no interest to the people that set priorities, those same people recognize it is imbedded in the culture of the department or perhaps even the company. However, resolving process and organization dilemmas are more recently recognized for reaping exponental saving as compared to other more easily quantified problems. Pam Parry in her book *"The Bottom Line"* 2000 lays out a business case for organizing a company to an international standard. Taking a different approach, but achieving equal or greater results the work Mikel Harry and Richard Schroeder, have done on achieving quality and efficiency by scrutinizing processes in their book *Six Sigma, The Breakthrough Management Strategy Revolutionizing The World's Top Corporations 2006* adds another perspective held by many successful companies today. I mention these works to illustrate that business leaders and managers regard these seemingly mundane efforts important if not critical. This may be an instance where thoughtfully considering the big picture

Chapter 3. Engaging the Other Person

before asking questions about the assignment is helpful.

Our information organization opportunity can start with a vision of how things are elsewhere or what an effective file system should look like. The vision is what I referred to as the "Picture", only in this case it is probably more appropriate to call it "the big picture". We need to provide structure that will improve practices both dramatically and incrementally. Even though cultural changes are generally evolutionary not revolutionary dramatic changes will encourage other gradual changes. Feedback from all stakeholders to the information archives that are relied on by many people should follow an established and robust management system. The first rule for identifying a system should be to keep it simple.

Question what other people have done to resolve similar situations. Can you clearly define what needs to be done in your situation? Will the method improve the accuracy and precision of the information retrieval by system users? Can a casual user of the system see a relevance to other information systems? Did others approach to information management comprehend the breath and depth of your difficulty? Does your approach simplify logical retrieval and storage of information? Don't insist on reinventing the wheel if an off the shelf solution is applicable. At the very least build on what others have established and add to it your custom solution that meets your needs.

Engaging the other person is a bit of an understatement, as you can see, rarely a single person needs to be addressed. Many people

Chapter 3. Engaging the Other Person

and more often than not organizations may need to be part of your consideration when you begin an engagement. If you start with the primary contact as a starting point and let the task before you determine where you go next. Keep your approach simple and make what your next step is clear to your supporters.

One way to improve your communication with supporters and resources you need to recruit is through a presentation. Which of the tools mentioned so far will most likely communicate quickly and accurately the ideas you need to share? If you haven't guessed by now it is the picture. Why the picture? It can in a single frame communicate ownership for a multitude of people or organizations. Remember how important ownership is to your ability to contribute, well if others feel a sense of ownership they are far more likely to contribute to your vision. Diagrams or flowcharts don't require a degree in art, but they do require you to think through your proposal.

As you analyze the picture you paint for other people consider their needs. What are others looking to accomplish that your project or effort could help them achieve? Is there a synergy that others could benefit from as a result of collaborating with you and others within the group of resources you hope to tap? What are the costs? Who pays what for the cost burden? Will your effort encourage teamwork? Sometimes the real synergy that is derived is a sense of teamwork that can be tapped in the future for other challenges that have been identified, but not yet initiated.

First impressions are important and as image consultant

Chapter 3. Engaging the Other Person

Michelle Sterling states "non-verbal communication encompasses 93% of our overall message" in her message to entrepreneurs at http://entrepreneurs.about.com/cs/marketing/a/uc062003.htm . Michelle Sterling breaks it down this way, "In our professional and personal lives, we'd like to think we could make friends and influence people if we verbally articulate our message with optimism, enthusiasm, charisma, poise and charm. However, did you know that verbal impact of communication only accounts for 7% of your overall message? The bulk of our communication comes across in our appearance and body language, comprising 55%. Tone, speed and inflection of our voice make up the remaining 38%." Michelle's suggest greater consideration of your image or how people "picture" you as the messenger. I agree preparing for your appearance is a valuable piece of what needs to be considered to make that first impression a good one. Principally, because that picture people develop of you will tend to become a large part of what they take away from a single meeting. Secondly consider the message will be what ultimately needs to be considered and may be the core of your credibility regarding any subject you may present to potential supporters.

If the presentation needs to quickly gain acceptance consider what questions you need to answer at the meeting. Do you have people on hand that can put to rest questions that impact the additional planning, funding, resources that are needed to implement this idea through the first operational stage? Remember you need to bring something to the party besides good looks. Proposals that are vying for implementation meet greater resistance, because they are more likely to create change. The core of what you need to provide is a vision that addresses the discomfort that these changes create. Regardless of how great an idea is, failing to address the difficulty of transition is more likely to sabotage your effort to gain acceptance than the idea itself. Most people would acknowledge that the project will evolve as it encounters difficulty during implementation. Here is where the vision needs to be clear on how these difficulties will be resolved in a rapid and rational manner.

Some of the sayings by well known people will probably apply when you're developing a vision. Yogi Berra was credited with saying, "You got to be careful if you don't know where you're going, because you might not get there." Another saying credited to Ben Franklin states: "By failing to prepare, you prepare to fail." Believe me when I say there are more sayings like those that tend to provide fair warning and no comfort for those people that would ignore the need to spend time thinking through ideas they would propose to others.

Just as your values are important when it comes to identifying information worth saving, so others values need consideration when proposing changes that will seem worth making to them. As you prepare to present ideas consider your role as it is perceived by other people. Are you accepted as an agent of change, or are you more a part of the current bureaucracy that perpetuates the status quo? You may have ownership of what needs to be presented, but are you the

Chapter 3. Engaging the Other Person

best person to present the idea? Maybe it is a job for an unbiased facilitator. Remember some of those cautions Michelle Sterling provided and how the message is impacted by the presenter. The needs of other people are no more in focus than when it comes to their perception of the event and the presenter.

Most managers are rewarded for cost savings, so start by detailing some of the cost savings each of the individuals or department can expect as a result of changes you propose. Costs can be material savings, personnel, or simply time. Most managers would agree to changes that simply take the complexity out of any existing process, because it makes management of the process easier for them and their personnel. If you encounter resistance to change try to negotiate making change on a more gradual basis.

Remember we started out trying to engage the other person in an effort better manage information. This led us to reviewing how we present our ideas to others and how they are received. We further had to consider negotiating change that may need the combined effort of many other people. Even though it may seem like we have strayed a long distance from our initial goal, it is this connection between information and other people's lives that can make managing information difficult.

Many people that are particularly good at the mechanics of information management have some difficulty engaging other people. This is a similar phenomenon to engineers that are moved into management positions, but are not good people managers. It does not

Chapter 3. Engaging the Other Person

mean that those of us that enjoy the intricacies of the personal computers and the power of the internet are doomed to stay in the shadows. Instead it is just a reason to exercise those less than developed people skills that are needed to be an effective manager of information.

While working for the Chrysler Corporation as a technical instructor I was asked to provide a class that reviewed fundamentals of geometric tolerance controls for a skilled trades group in Canada. It proved to be a rather challenging week as instructor. This was a group of skilled trades people that were keenly aware of how company money was being spent for their training. They were very sensitive to any training that did not translate into visible improvements today.

During that first day they had serious questions about the usefulness of the information I was there to provide. I explained that it was general information that was a part of materials they were expected to understand in the workplaces throughout the plant. I challenged them to take that last hour of the day to revisit their workplaces and collect the drawings and other samples of information they were expected to understand and bring it to class the next day.

When they returned the next day they had bundles of drawings, sketches and booklets they worked with everyday. Together we sifted and sorted through them arranging them in a way that would allow us to address different aspects one at a time over the next four days.

This required a lot of additional work on my part to address their concerns about that weeks' training, but they were right and

Chapter 3. Engaging the Other Person

when we came to the end of the week we all conceded that a lot had been learned by tailoring the instruction to their specific needs. They were also grateful that someone finally listened.

Managing information effectively will generally require treating people with respect and likewise respecting the information that they may contribute to the base of all other information. It does not mean that you must agree with their perspective, but instead respect their ownership of the ideas they choose to elaborate and defend. Despite your respect of a persons words and their quoted statements, don't be surprised if an interpretation of those words generates an argument. Some people insist that you only ascribe the highest ethical and moral meanings to their words regardless how outlandish their statements might strike the average person. That singular fact makes your analysis and scrutiny of what you choose to save and make a part of any report very important.

How have people in the past chosen to analyze information? If analysis was a business effort there is a chance that the analysis used some objective criteria, but that isn't necessarily true. Businesses like other organizations are comprised of the same people that in their private life can't seem to separate fact from fiction, so unless the business promotes objective business analysis the results may be no better than the people with the assignment. Fortunately, most people that are asked to do analysis for business purposes have shown some ability in that direction.

Business analysis usually starts with the hard information that

Chapter 3. Engaging the Other Person

has been provided by the information source. The information provided by any source can be viewed skeptically especially if the source is apt to profit by your acceptance of that information as fact. Second and third party validation is usually a minimum requirement. Testimonials from satisfied customers are a common offering when a company is asked to validate the product or service it has to sell, but most large companies require much more than testimonials.

What better than a satisfied customer? An answer to that question is objective and measurable criteria that review the advertised benefits the product or service will deliver. If a product is advertised to improve cardiovascular health a testimonial does not demonstrate the same results a treadmill test may yield. If a service boasts that the company has skilled workers a testimonial will not present the credentials of the people that provide the service. We can conclude that customer testimonials are nice, but there needs to be some review preferably by a third party that does not have a stake in the prosperity of the company to review what the company provides for a customer. It would also be helpful if the company had some kind of ranking relative to other competing companies.

Much of that work has been done for customers of large organizations when the organizations make it on the list of companies that do nothing but evaluate companies and their products. Usually these rating services are available to the public for a small fee. What about medium and small companies that may offer great value at a very reasonable price? Perhaps greater attention to detail is warranted when a customer evaluates small business. Where do we get information on small companies that we can trust? Small companies depend on responsible individuals that have paid the price of admission to be in the market and have not created any bad experiences for customers. Potential customers can use the Better Business Bureau, Credit Reports and Background Checks on the individuals that run the operation. Some of these services come at a price, but it is a known price that gives you confidence ahead of any purchase agreement that may obligate you to much more money.

Large corporations have established a screening process that evaluates the financial status of a prospective vendor along with the companies' assets and business processes. They do this in an effort to avoid disasters from occurring in the middle of an on going project after a vendor has been approved. Some general approach is needed to evaluate all vendors equally.

A method that I would indorse as covering all of the basics is referred to as "Critical Thinking". This is a way of thinking that tends to subject the product or service, to a level of scrutiny that filters out products and services that are poorly defined, have little detail, are without measurable numbers, can't be compared to others, don't have proper references or credentials and fail to satisfy logical conclusions.

CHAPTER 4

Analysis of Key Information

When we analyze we hope to identify patterns, trends, and possibly root causes. Analysis requires you take an active role, reviewing the information as it is presented or as it is cataloged or even when it is retrieved to be reused. Without being able to readily retrieve information analysis is slowed and even interrupted. Analysis requires you shuffle information to find logical combinations. When information is coming in, catalog it, review it, and analyze it using "Critical Thinking", so the retrieval and reuse of it is less difficult.

Cataloging information is analysis at the highest level. You only need to identify the category the information applies to and separate it for further consideration. Think in terms of your favorite catalog to browse. Can you easily distinguish from your collection of information the page most likely to contain what you are looking for without an endless search? Establishing the categories ahead of your collection effort is recommended. You can always create some

Chapter 4. Analysis of Key Information

categories for unexpected information as they occur, but any preparation ahead of time simplifies what needs to be done. Try to employ a numbering system that allows you to expand on your cataloging effort. If you have extensive information to collect the Dewey Decimal System may be what you need. "The Dewey Decimal Classification (DDC) system, devised by library pioneer Melvil Dewey in the 1870s and owned by OCLC since 1988, provides a dynamic structure for the organization of library collections. Now in its 22nd edition, and available in print and Web versions, the DDC is the world's most widely used library classification system," http://www.oclc.org/dewey/about/default.htm . Start with the simplest approach first unless you anticipate volumes of information will be cataloged.

Next some review during collection is appropriate, if a break in the action occurs. Reviewing helps you clean up your cataloging effort and begin to do some analysis during the collection process. Review it alone or review it with others, collaboration may provide additional perspectives worth noting as you continue to build your collection for more rigorous analysis. Consider these review forums

- Formal meetings
- Informal Reviews
    - At the coffee machine or water cooler
    - Working Lunch
    - Limited workplace discussions

If the topic is variance of mathematical models it will probably fall

Chapter 4. Analysis of Key Information

outside of interesting lunch time topics, so be careful not to review information that has no audience.

Cataloging is expected to break down information so it can be retrieved or referenced by the analysis yet to come. All libraries and information databases wait for someone with a purpose to unlock the value that the information contains. Any single purpose can use analysis to identify patterns or trends to find and eliminate root causes of problem situations. Communicating with other team members informally or formally and identifying their needs with yours will yield the nuggets of wisdom you hope to use to serve the original purpose of your analysis.

Formal reviews that follow an agenda are best done in modules, because the people you may call on are the same people that will review the final product. Keeping the information brief and narrow in scope helps keep the individuals asked to review interested. Remember everybody has only so many hours to contribute to your effort, when you exceed that limit you may put them at odds with you for reasons unrelated to the ideas that are being shared. The best review is one that serves your purpose and the person invited, so when you assemble the guest list keep their interests and current projects in mind. The agenda can include others interest to the extent it is manageable within the time limits of your meeting.

Informal reviews around the "water cooler" that give you an opportunity to address questions others may have after a formal review allow you to cement a better connection with people you may need in

Chapter 4. Analysis of Key Information

the future to support rational for a business case. The informal meeting may allow you to ask questions that were too department specific to be addressed in a cross functional team meeting. Above all else let people know your open to ideas that would benefit a wider group of people while not significantly changing the scope of your original purpose.

How do current patterns or trends support your direction or proposed change? Are there greater forces at work beyond the walls of your business that will support change in the direction you would take the organization you work for or lead? Be detailed and numerous in your response to these questions, because the answer may determine who chooses to share your vision going forward.

There are times when your work or business environment seems to be functioning well despite what is reported by others in the same industry. Regardless of what planning has insulated you from, if business deteriorates significantly the impact of the outside world may visit without warning. Making yourself aware of the pressures in your business sector and problems plaguing your business competitors is only reasonable awareness. Connections to the reality of the current business environment may rally support for new ideas that address meaningful changes. Do the changes you propose improve a product, service or operation of your business at a reasonable cost in a short period of time?

The message you develop from any analysis must be brief enough to be remembered and lengthy enough to have substance. A

Chapter 4. Analysis of Key Information

message that rambles on about detail of a proposal may have greater value when details are requested. I would encourage a message that captures the imagination and only hints at the detail. Build support for your ideas a step at a time in presentations that introduce new ideas or new direction. Develop presentations that keep the attention of the audience from start to finish. Even if you are not presenting details be prepared to provide details if the audience insists on your filling in the blanks.

The audience will ask for detail and timelines as they grow to accept the direction as their own. As an idea gains acceptance it creates a sense of urgency for results that were used to sell the idea. If the claims made were too good to be true people will rethink their support, so be careful not to inflate the merits of what your proposed change will bring. Keep the rewards simple to describe and easy to measure. The analysis that yields information must inform people to the extent they question your proposal.

Analysis has a way of making you aware of limited action you can take without any formal approval that will bolster your argument for positive change without delay. Do not overlook the obvious things you could be doing without approval. People with a different perspective are likely to point to those items and suggest you start with the small items and dismiss your larger concern. Go a step further and ask for others to identify waste or inefficiency that is apparent to them from their perspective. This is not to suggest you do things in a haphazard fashion, but instead unearth what can be done to improve a system in a systematic way.

As you learn to manage and use information, it will be useful to evaluate the same information critically. Although an extensive review of "Critical Thinking" would take us beyond the scope of this book, it is useful to review a description and some fundamental elements Roy Eichhorn, of the Strategic Systems Department Army Management Staff College Fort Belvoir, VA, outlines at http://www.amsc.belvoir.army.mil/roy.html. As he states "Today, a number of definitions of thinking and of critical thinking in particular exist in academia. That multiple definitions exist is not unusual when one considers the field of inquiry." Roy Eichorn further states in his abstract titled *Developing Thinking Skills: Critical Thinking At The Army Management Staff College*, that "Critical thinking is the ability to be in control of one's thinking. It includes the ability to consciously examine the elements of one's reasoning, or that of another, and evaluate that reasoning against universal intellectual standards - clarity, accuracy, precision, relevance, depth, breadth, and logic." Roy Eichorn goes on to give credit for the definition used to "The Universal Intellectual Standards from Linda Elder and Richard Paul (1996)." Thinking critically about information is useful in several ways, first to separate information coming in, second to analyze information for use and third when you choose to reuse information as a basis to act. Understanding how the information you collect, analyze and use will influence how you act. It will give you greater confidence in the decisions you make.

Chapter 4. Analysis of Key Information

I have heard this definition of "Critical Thinking" used before by others and while not knowing the origin I used it to a guide my analysis of information, because the definition seemed simple and easy to accomplish. All that I needed to remember were seven words, Clarity, Accuracy, Precision, Relevance, Depth, Breath, and Logic to dig into the detail of any topic, or to quickly analyze information on the fly. Now much more needs to be considered during analysis, but some application of this version of "Critical Thinking" will guide the real time and posthumous analysis that needs to be done if you are to unlock the value of information.

Our first contact with the source of information can be the most important, because a missed step here may derail or deny the analysis yet to come. Here it is important to be as good a listener as your personality will allow you to be. Interrupting a speaker before they are able to answer a question does a disservice to your effort to get valued information. Focus on establishing "clarity" or a single statement that summarizes the speakers point. Sometimes you may need to be assertive when the answer begins to go well beyond the scope of your question. Actively listen and paraphrase the speakers answer in a context that is relevant to you, if the speaker verifies your application it helps to move on. Look for opportunities that the speaker provides when they conclude a thought or emphasize a point to engage the speaker for purposes of either taking the discussion deeper or moving on to a related topic.

Chapter 4. Analysis of Key Information

Next establish "accuracy" or some measurable observable definition the speaker has provided to define their position. Can you restate that definition in a way that the speaker will agree with you? As you establish accuracy, it is equally important to include "precision" or limits on the application of a statement. Does the accuracy you have established apply under all conditions or are there limits? If there are limits define the limits. Here is an example of a statement that is accurate but not precise. Sharks must keep moving to breathe. Does this include all sharks? How much movement is needed? These are questions that need to be answered if the statement about sharks is to be both accurate and precise.

It is that first engagement where some of the best analysis happens, because it may involve several people informally brainstorming an idea. The others may have differing perspectives that help you review the information in ways you may not have considered. Certainly some time can be wasted, but generally these engagements add value to any information you will collect. Earlier I mentioned that the focus of collecting data needs to be on what is observable and measurable. Collecting the literal remarks of individuals will collect both raw data and analytical insights. Carrying forward the quoted statements helps provide perspective for people that were not present. What was the breath and depth of the discussion? Define the scope of the discussion to get breathe and depth. When doing analysis, the clarity of earlier statements, accuracy of information shared and the precision of all information is critical to

Chapter 4. Analysis of Key Information

the analysis that may lead to plans and action. Using "Critical Thinking" fundamentals include any noted relevance or logic that adds value to the information that is first presented or brainstormed during discussion with other people.

Be open and engaging with people that are likely to have information you need. An engaging person is far more likely to hear valued facts, than is a cool aloof stranger. It doesn't take a whole lot of effort to create an impression in either direction, so work quickly to engage others giving them a willing listener and a sounding board for their perspective. The choice of topics can be yours provided they share an interest in the topic. Listening to the depth and breath of what others have to say may be a key to the relevance and logic that needs to be derived.

Finally contribute to the discussion to avoid one word answers to questions you may need answered. Facilitate the contributions of others that contribute freely. A conversation needs to move two ways if it is to persist. Some people will contribute volumes, but if they grow weary you need to be ready to energize the conversation to allow more time to solicit a position or more facts. A one way conversation can quickly go sour leaving you alone and avoided by others. If you are trying to derive the logic of someone's decisions you will need to conversely ask logical questions. Nothing is more irritating than someone asking questions that lack an apparent connection to previous questions and answers.

What happens after the meeting has ended? Analysis done

Chapter 4. Analysis of Key Information

after an encounter is usually done to determine the next step. Providing analysis that other people support is important. Using trusted sources of information to draw conclusions that decision makers need to endorse helps facilitate negotiating a direction many people support. The decision to take a direction may only be in the hands of one person, but following the direction needs the full support of the staff and employees to move quickly to achieve lasting results. Large organizations usually have higher levels of politics that rule the decision making process.

Some years ago while working on a contract basis as a designer for the Ford Motor Company I was asked to engage the hourly workforce that would either install, maintain or use the machine being modified before finalizing the design. This proved to take a fair amount of analysis over and above the task of just making a change that met the engineer specifications. The result however was a new configuration that the entire workforce supported in production. The contributions did not change the estimated costs, but did add some features that made the machinery simple to install and service.

Collaboration has a funny way of engaging a wide range of people that would have never met except for the common purpose that brings them together. While working at the Chrysler Corporation in the mid 1980s' on an Interactive Video Project I was asked to attend a computer conference in Chicago. It just so happened I learned about a relatively new database company that had caught my attention at the conference, because of the relational databases they could develop from a fairly simple code. I brought a sample back and discussed the merits of the approach this company took, but was told we already had a way to build relational databases.

Some years later in the late 1990s' I was developing a prototype database application for the General Motors Corporation and to my surprise the database that held the majority of all data was a product of the same company that I met back in the 1980's. Oracle had become the database engine of choice due to the open computer code that had so impressed me so many years earlier.

As I learned more about the developments from then until now it reawakened my enthusiasm for the product and what it would enable our business group to do in a relatively short period of time. Those old discussions that examined the possibilities were now about to become reality more than ten years later with an entirely different business group.

As I discussed the options we had, I found a very enthusiastic management that was not aware of the desktop tools currently available at all workstations that would accommodate what I proposed. This lead to a prototype development that later was to become a larger project that a vendor would oversee. Hours, days and years of collaboration sprung from only a few simple departmental meetings. The open collaboration between employees and vendors made this project a success.

The level of difficulty increases with the size of the organization. Analysis needs to include stakeholders that will be impacted by decisions made. Reaching out to the organization helps determine the depth and breathe of opportunities for improvement ahead of making any decision on new direction. Analysis may not establish a consensus of opinion, but it should support decisions that need to be made on direction and commitment that are waiting for the analysis.

What level of commitment do you bring with you? Are you acting as committed as you would have others act. What risk have you created for yourself? If you are playing it safe and expecting everyone else to take the risk you are not leading the way. Some risk taking on your part can be attractive if you have demonstrated that it leads to success. Analysis is not a separate and distinct area of work, but instead an integral part of making things happen that will affect positive change. There are many moving parts to a system you may be trying to change so keep the larger perspective in mind as you provide analysis for other decision makers. Earlier I mentioned how some simple tools could be used to collect information. The very same tools are easily applied to the task of analysis.

The "question" not only helps identify specific facts, but reveals earlier rational for past decisions. If the rational for past decisions is no longer valid, what has changed? Building support for new decision will include answering many questions based on the past. Analysis begins early and often in the collection process. You make determinations about the value and relevance of information as it relates to your assignment. Does the information take you a step

Chapter 4. Analysis of Key Information

closer to answering some ultimate question that needs to be answered? Does the information have some factual basis considering the references of the speaker or the sources documented along the way? What are the observable and measurable pieces of information that you can retrieve for consideration by others? Are there price options that depend on quantity or season of the year?

Picture or visualize the proposed opportunities and benefits that flow from proposed changes that depend on information you need to collect. Is this image a shared vision or is it just in the mind of the presenter? A shared vision can expedite moving the largest of organizations through change quickly. Is the new vision supported by tested models that are accepted by other people in the organization? Pictures, models or shared visions communicate large amounts or information in small amounts of time. Collecting information that reinforces the vision or that clearly identifies other considerations that need to be made ahead of large commitments is critical. Use communications that include pictures literally or figuratively to leave lasting impressions that reinforce verbal or written communication. The analysis that includes pictures provides a perspective that is more easily understood and recalled.

Organized analysis done by one person or 100 people over time is always more effective than analysis called for on a moments notice. Thinking through an agenda or objectives helps lead analysis to conclusions that decision makers need to consider. Here is another instance where that old saying "It's the thought that counts" makes sense. When it comes to collecting information, your thinking ahead, thinking during the process and thinking after you have collected a quantity of information may seem obvious, but is not always done.

Clear thoughts defined by accurate and precise detail are a goal of analysis, so conducting meetings that may ramble aimlessly require an agenda. The agenda is more than a list of related topics, it must introduce the breath and depth of the subject to ensure the solution is robust. Robust solutions are marked by the ability to satisfy a wide cross section of customers at many levels of the organization. Taking action to finalize analysis may require ownership of a project or process. Soliciting volunteers or assigning ownership may be the action needed to advance toward the goal that should have been identified early in the information gathering project.

Does your analysis include statistical references that support conclusions? Why is analysis being done? Are your answers clear, accurate and precise? Does your analysis identify relevant and logical direction with breath and depth?

Triage is a word used by medical people to describe a process for separating and prioritizing medical conditions. Anyone that must manage large amounts of information in a fast moving environment must learn to apply triage to engaging the flow of information. Certainly information may flow heaviest when it is presented, but during analysis information is fleeting like fire flies and may not be scripted, making it more difficult to capture. Analysis requires facilitation to extract and record. Analysis must lay the foundation for

Chapter 4. Analysis of Key Information

profitable use of the information. Has data been collected and analyzed, to solve a problem, lead an initiative or some other purpose? Recall the purpose that precipitated collecting and analyzing the information. The purpose will drive the analysis.

Managing and using information can be tedious but rewarding. Efficient access to information that allows rapid analysis and the development of improvement plans result in improved business processes or personal decisions and present endless opportunities. Some analysis may require that new information discovered during the analysis be attached, referenced or otherwise embedded in the core data. Some of the new information may be hypothesis or conclusions based on discussions or experiments. These pieces of information should be the logic that helps rationalize change.

The analysis needs to serve the original purpose and rationalize the expense of changes as cost effective. Presenting this information is important to the people that need to plan for change. Will the changes be revolutionary or evolutionary? How strong is the analysis? Are there examples of others that have engaged similar change? Although the questions you ask yourself can be endless as you lead or participate in analysis, drop back to satisfying the purpose originally set forward for the analysis. Limit your analysis to those seven words that will distinguish the analysis from an unorganized approach. Spend time establishing clarity, accuracy, precision, relevance, depth, breadth, and logic. The analysis that seemed like a never ending string of questions and answers should provide a supporting document that

Chapter 4. Analysis of Key Information

delivers insight and opportunity to the decision maker.

The analysis may also have revealed some patterns, trends or even root causes of problems that suggest the need for change. It is important that these patterns, trends and root causes be included in your presentation, but you must include the supporting information that will probably be challenged. The current status was put in place by someone and if they are still present they are likely to challenge changes that suggest decision making errors were made in the past. The information may identify how change over time has made otherwise good decisions obsolete.

During the analysis phase of your process do not overlook recording or storing the conclusions. Storage of information is important, because to make presentations you need to retrieve the results of all the leg work you have done that makes your information worth reporting. Certainly use all the latest gadgets and devices to format the information, but reserve the space between your ears for storing the passion you feel for your conclusions. When you present your ideas communicating your passion is not something that is easily scripted. So unless you have a famous playwright developing your dialogue, review it in your mind and store it there for future use.

Patterns, trends and root causes can be very powerful when making a point, but be careful that you can provide details that back up your claims. Illustrate how a new pattern or trend can be changed incrementally. The same measurement you used to identify the current status may be used to determine any progress after a change is

Chapter 4. Analysis of Key Information

adopted. The question is, can the information you provide hold up to the same scrutiny that you have used on other information and results? Projections you provide will be subject to the same scrutiny that may discredit current operations. New projections are needed to support an argument to change the status quo. Without performance projections you put the burden of information retrieval and analysis on the audience. The audience wants to make changes that make a difference, but they need evidence of success. Provide your audience with what they need to make a decision today. Experimental prototypes can be very useful when presenting a new method or product, because it answers feasibility and functionality questions that might not be answered any other way.

Remember how I stressed that first impressions are lasting and important? Well the presentation of the analysis is another one of those first impressions. If the analysis creates more questions than it answers it will not provide the insight or the opportunity the decision maker is looking for to make a decision and move on to the next step.

When you review your presentation ask yourself, could I make a decision that may impact my assets based on the information presented? What level of risk does this decision require and is the risk clearly defined? Are decision makers that match the level of risk in the room or should this review be digested at a lower level and then carried to the next level for an approval? How time sensitive are decisions that need to be made? All of these questions and probably some others need to be considered in preparation for any presentation to decision makers.

Another way to think of presentations that are trying to solicit support is to think of the presentation as a "trial" and you are the advocate of your position. Any attorney worth hiring would probably have researched many alternatives to their position before they present it. As an advocate you are required to do some deep thinking of scenarios that might block progress or even deny changes you propose be accomplished.

In the business world a good idea can move quickly toward implementation if it considers both the people that need to make the decision and the risks that it subjects the organization to if things do not go as originally planned. Backup plans and alternatives that support going forward despite need for change are a practical approach to planning. Leaders like having options.

Equally as important as risk of failure is the opportunity of success. What benefits will flow from change that is put in place? To the extent you can articulate the benefits will be the extent to which you build an attractive alternative to business as usual. Here again a plan for reaping the rewards of the changes made need to be articulated. Is the return on investment (ROI) expected in a week, a month, one year or longer?

Spell it out, detailing the range of return on investment you expect on a monthly basis. Most times the benefits will fuel the attraction to the changes you propose. Benefits may include intangibles that improve the flow of work, but nothing attracts

Chapter 4. Analysis of Key Information

potential owners quicker than financial benefits that improve the company bottom line.

Try to present your ideas in as many forums as possible to add impact through diversity. Most ideas that eventually gain acceptance will need a wide base of support. Start early and hone your message as it gains momentum. Even if the gains the company can reap are a narrow financial windfall. All elements of the company benefit from a better bottom line at the end of the year.

Here is a real world example of how analysis helped me move an effort that had made no progress for one year off of dead center. The Chrysler Corporation had purchased 100 kiosks for the purpose of delivering safety training. The effort was a total success and had saved the corporation a large amount of money due to the efficiency of the delivery system. The new effort envisioned the same 100 kiosks delivering a wider variety of training in addition to the health and safety training.

The first plan was to ask a number of companies to compete for the job of supplying new programs that would run on the original 100 kiosks. While that effort was being pursued I bought a system identical to the 100 the corporation had purchased. It was interesting to study the computer code and speculate how vendors would integrate their products. To the Corporations surprise we could not find another vendor to modify our machines to run their programs. Instead they would insist we would need to replace all of the hardware to accommodate their products. The search went on for a little more than a year.

After learning what made the original system tick I proposed we buy the vendors products with rights to repurpose them for our equipment. This idea was not proposed before doing a great deal of analysis that would ensure it could be done. After a year of soliciting many vendors that said it could not be done resistance to an in-house effort would be high. The sales vehicle for this effort needed to be a working prototype that made it clear that this was an achievable goal.

The prototype was one of the 100 kiosks with added capability. Applying all I had learned over the past year on my personal system was put to practical use in developing a prototype that demonstrated that our in-house effort could move our department toward a goal that had eluded us for over a year. The new configuration allowed for stepping off to new programs while leaving the original program in place. This all seems rather elementary in today's world, but this was a system that was put together in 1986 before Microsoft Windows or the Internet existed for the average computer.

As a result of doing the analysis needed and developing a working prototype the proposal and the project was widely accepted and a resounding success that consumed the efforts of the department for several years to come.

CHAPTER 5

Where did I leave that chart?

How many times has a presenter said, where did I leave that chart? Presenting detail that supports the analysis in a way that can be quickly communicated is essential to capturing the imagination and passion of others. Charts are pictures that save many words. Charts communicate detail through a visual channel and can generate support for the direction that the analysis suggests.

The classic example of someone that became famous for his charts was Ross Perot. An article "Perot Begins Campaign, on TV, With charts" by James Brooke appeared in the New York Times September 2, 1996 describes how Ross Perot spent thirty minutes making his point that there is no "Free Candy". Although Ross Perot was unsuccessful in his bid for President, he did receive an enormous portion of the vote despite his third party status. I can't help thinking how those charts that simplified government spending and poor results found their mark with some voters.

Information that accompanies the analysis should neutralize

bias and support clear direction based on an objective measurable facts. Analysis may need champions for opposing views. The champions that are chosen or emerge should be responsible for their own charts, because ultimately they will be called on to sell their rational for a specific plan. Rendering objective conclusions or a balanced set of arguments may require more time or resources, but acting on bad analysis can be more expensive long term. Here again originators or people explaining the analysis need to be clear, accurate and precise when communicating. Using charts can be very powerful when championing a specific recommendation for change.

It is advisable to attach independent analysis of similar studies to either contrast in-house analysis or support it. Independent analysis may not be entirely free of bias itself, if it supports products the company doing the analysis sells. When purchasing analysis identify firms that have a reputation to protect. Analysis may not include all original data to allow drawing your own conclusions. Companies that have worked hard and long to achieve a good reputation are less likely to squander it for the price of a single analysis.

If all of the analysis is done in-house entertain more than one perspective. People from the same department that have different functions may see the same facts differently. An inter-department prospectus may not be an option even if it may yield a better analysis to attach to the original information.

If you're personally working on taking a new direction and the analysis is yours alone it can still be objective. Use other people to

Chapter 5. Where did I leave that chart?

sound out your ideas on. Read books that are written by people in similar circumstances. Most people are surprised to find out their life and special circumstances are not as unique as originally thought. Interestingly books may present some of your information, analysis and plans for change in ways that make it easy to evaluate the results.

Charts are not simply bars and graphs with associated numbers. Charts can include cartoons that use humor to make a point where the picture communicates many words. Be very careful when adding video or audio to a presentation. There are 1000 bad examples for every one good example of how video and audio are used. Probably the best examples are found among commercial advertisements.

For those people that are not artistically inclined simply outsource the art work and stick to appraising the impact. So many times there are artistic people within a team that have not been identified. Simply ask the question; "Is there anyone that can help?" Remember the objective is to communicate a point clearly quickly and in a way that people are likely to remember. Cartoon characters give anonymity to people that are best left unidentified. Focus on correcting a broken process instead of fixing people that are all too human.

Gage the success of your presentation by the remarks and references that persist long after the presentation. If it was a success people will associate their remarks with the elements that they most enjoyed. Likewise negative remarks may be associated with any flat spots or awkward moments. Asking for formal evaluations may not be the best way of surveying an audience. Instead of a questionnaire have an informal discussion at the end of your presentation that identifies questions that were not answered or not answered fully. You might have a meeting a week later to discuss what people think after having some time to think the ideas over for a while.

Some presenters are skilled at expanding their presentation on the fly, but don't do this if it extends the normal schedule of events, because it will seem too tedious and rambling. Clear concise points that pass the time quickly leaving people wanting more is the best approach.

Charts are another way to create memorable pictures that simply take too many words to convey. It is just as important for people to remember what you said as it is that you say it. If there is wisdom in what you have to say, do everything possible to find ways for people to remember what you said. If you can get people to use something more than one channel to receive your message, there is a greater probability that they will recall your message.

Here are some practical approaches to creating charts for any presentation, from the bar room napkin to the jumbo screen at the 1000 plus seat convention.

- Identify the purpose you are trying to satisfy
- Do your Homework
- Create a Structure
- Identify the material that will cover the structure
- Identify the elements that need a chart or visual aid

Chapter 5. Where did I leave that chart?

- Keep charts to a minimum
- Stay focused
- Use local or purchased talent to create charts
- Make your point

You might not have expected this many bulleted points, but consider that charts only complement a position that has been carefully thought out before it is presented.

If your presentation has purpose it is much easier to engage the audience. Is your purpose to save money, make money, improve quality, or improve the quality of life? Make it clear up front what you are trying to accomplish. A clear purpose attracts energy for discussion. If you neglect the purpose it will be the question the audience may use to discredit your entire effort.

Most ideas for change are not new despite what you may think even as you champion positive change. Doing your homework before you propose change is a first step. Review the efforts of other people that had similar approaches to the same problem. We learn from the mistakes of others as much or more than we learn from our own mistakes. The lengthy efforts of others can provide a wealth of support for what you may propose.

Many ideas that may seem spontaneous are in fact ideas that have been reviewed hundreds and thousands of times before they make their way to a napkin type proposal. After numerous iterations that explore the options of a proposal, a single line of thinking emerges on to paper in a way that other people can appraise. When the

Chapter 5. Where did I leave that chart?

idea emerges some people would say how simple, but those who have experience realize the amount of effort that lead to the simple solution.

Create a structure that provides logic for other people as well as yourself. Structure is important early in any discussion, because it allows others to follow your thinking. Structure allows you to identify what needs more explanation and what may need a chart. Structure can be a way for you to find holes or weak spots in your thinking that need additional consideration. Outlines and summary statements assist the search for information that provides the glue between ideas that support positive change.

The elements that need charts are usually those that take too many words to explain. There may be a number of interactions that are just too complicated to describe in words. A visual illustrates the connection in a moment. Don't overlook the opportunity to include humor or other entertaining elements that make a tedious review less tense.

One of my pet peeves is endless charts. If your presentation is one hour it does not mean you need 60 charts. The portion of your presentation that needs charts may revolve around two or three basic charts. If you do more with less people are more inclined to remember what you presented. Remember that time can be spent during a presentation answering some questions that will increase interest in what is yet to be presented. An easy way to do this is to ask the anticipated questions that some people may have as part of the presentation.

Chapter 5. Where did I leave that chart?

Stay focused and don't forget your purpose as you present your ideas. Your presentation should support your purpose from start to finish. Reinforce the purpose to avoid wandering off on a tangent. Repeating your purpose helps focus the audience and may make them more receptive to ideas you present.

Use local or purchased talent to prepare charts. The key word here is "talent". If you add sloppy unprofessional charts to an otherwise stunning presentation you may sabotage your purpose. Look inside your own organization for people that have provided chart creation services for other successful projects in your company that can be enlisted in your effort. Don't make your presentation a time to present new untested talent.

Finally, make your point or simply repeat it in a way that attracts people to your perspective. Give them a reason to agree. What is in the change you propose that will provide the audience benefits or value? Most people want to be associated with sound ideas that make positive changes, so when you determine your purpose evaluate it from the audiences' perspective. Would you support someone that brought a similar message to you? Is the idea clearly presented and easy to measure for success?

Are there any reasons to avoid charts? Yes, there are a few reasons that make charts of all kinds inappropriate. I can't remember any sermon that ever included charts. Certainly there is a lot of information to be considered, but generally sermons would not be improved by the presence of any number of charts.

Chapter 5. Where did I leave that chart?

Orators that are interested in an emotional connection with the audience would not be served by adding charts to their presentation. The most recent and best example of this is the 2008 political campaigns. Barack Obama being a good orator is drawing people to his message like a sermon. He would loose some charisma if he added charts into his discussion that looks to build an emotional connection with the audience. Hillary Clinton however, would be bolstered by charts that support the detail she claims her opponent is unwilling to furnish. It would add a visual channel to her presentation, and reinforce the points she is trying to make with words only. The other political party might not change the outcome either way by adding charts, because they all have balanced their messages between detail and oratory.

The danger any politician running for president would risk by using charts is that of being compared to Ross Perot and his famous chart talk. Ross Perot despite his popularity had many critics that cast him as a cartoon character. It would probably be political death of a national politician to have someone draw that comparison.

Senators, Congressmen and Congresswomen on both sides of the aisle regularly use charts with no fear of comparisons to Ross Perot. Given the difficulty of some of the issues they are working to address it is probably a good and effective use of charts. Anything that clarifies a politicians' position has got to be a good thing for the rest of us trying to make sense of what they are saying.

Speakers in general use charts to support logic and detail that otherwise do not seem to be connected. However when a speaker wants to close a sale they may dispense with all charts and use emotional dialogue to finally persuade the perspective buyer that buying the product now is the right thing to do. Many final sales don't depend on the presentation of honest comparisons, but depend on the customers' perception of the product.

When you go to a retail store generally the information you are presented with to make comparisons is price and packaging. Unless it is a fairly big item like an appliance no one is going to accompany you and present the merits of one product over another. It makes the consumers' job a little more difficult, because they need to make their comparison either by examining each product that minute or knowing what they want ahead of their visit to the retailer.

Retailers know this and will design packaging of products that carry their store name similar to competitors' products sitting on the same shelf. They try to make the sale by then showing a cost savings by brightly colored price tags on their products. It is all fair and legal, but it can be frustrating to the customer that has a favorite brand that isn't stocked or placed where it is easy to see.

Retailers do use charts when they want to direct you to a particular aisle or to a high margin product line. They will even add sales people to make the presentation if it helps move a profitable item. When you are getting generous service with any product consider what it might cost somewhere else. If price is important, there is probably a discounter somewhere with far less customer service. If the customer service is what you want, go no further make the purchase where the customer is valued.

The people that are explaining the benefits of one product over another regardless of any number of charts they might use are unlocking the value of information that is available. You may not have enough time to do all the research yourself, so you rely on these people to make presentations. Charts outside the business office take many different forms. Yard signs announcing home improvement being done or a political preference are all charts of one form or another. These charts are meant to inform us and hopefully persuade us to consider other options as we sort and sift through the many alternatives we have available to spend money on every day.

What is your experience? What are the charts in your life that vie for your attention every day? Make a list of the subtle and not so subtle examples. A chart can be a yellow label the size of a postage stamp or a billboard sign along the highway. The variety of charts and presentations is endless if you look closely at the way people make decisions. Consider the examples that have entered your life to get a sense of what influence they have on you.

Make a list of the types of decisions you have had to make, because it is when you need to make a decision that you will need to look for information that will help you decide. Then make a list of decisions you expect to make in the near future. Anticipating the need for information will help you organize your search for specific information.

Chapter 5. Where did I leave that chart?

Preparation for any event takes two forms fundamental preparation and technical preparation. Fundamental preparation requires you to learn basics like reading, writing and math. Technical preparation requires zeroing in on a very specific subject that you may not be aware of until you are asked to provide a solution, support a decision or new direction.

Over the years I have been responsible for developing charts that connect with large and small audiences. It would be helpful to review these real life examples that connected with intended audience and unlocked the value within the charted information. It is not easy to predict when you will be called on to use a chart that can make a difference as the following examples illustrate.

Some years ago when state government started to regulate automobile mechanics I had decided to take all the tests and gain certification as a Master Automobile Mechanic for the State of Michigan. It took a bit of study, but since I had worked on my own automobile for years all the systems were somewhat familiar. I received the certification and maintained it for several years although my primary work had nothing to do with repairing cars. This was fundamental preparation needed to address a wide range of questions.

As luck would have it I had one significant opportunity to make good use of my certification credential. A friend who later became my wife was having a great deal of trouble getting her new vehicle serviced. The problem was with the transmission and numerous trips to the dealership that never seemed to resolve the problem. I decided to research the manufacturers' specifications and dealer recommendations for repair. This was the technical preparation geared to find a recommended solution to a specific problem.

The research culminated in putting together a detailed troubleshooting log of the transmission problem. The log included references to all manufacturers' repair manuals and one chart that linked the manufacturers' recommendation that the transmission be replaced or rebuilt. I signed the documents and included my certification number to hopefully lend some credibility to the recommendation. When she made the next trip to the dealership she presented them my letter, log and chart of recommendations. She was pleasantly surprised that they quickly reviewed the information in my absence and replaced her transmission that never failed again.

From my perspective all the study and testing had been translated into a worthy presentation that moved the responsible party to do the right thing. It was a presentation that should not have been needed, but it came during a time when dealerships and manufacturers did not listen to customers. Customer service has come a long way since then and I never had occasion to make such a presentation since.

Another brief presentation I made some years later while working for a car manufacturer seemed to meet a similar and rather unexpected success. Meetings I previously attended never seemed as energetic as the one we held this day. Looking back on it now the key element was the chart.

Chapter 5. Where did I leave that chart?

While working for General Motors as a scheduler of tooling projects I had been asked to make a presentation to the management regarding efforts I was making to improve data management for our office work group. These early efforts were fundamental preparation to understanding the scope of the problem that needed resolution. Several of the reports we would assemble required hours of sifting and sorting through paper files with a great deal of redundant information. We needed to reduce the time this reporting effort took away from other worthwhile projects.

This was the best presentation I ever made and it used only one chart. That single chart referenced computer desktop tools that were in place and could be used that day to extend productivity of the entire office. Needless to say many people leaned forward in their seats anxious to know the name of these undiscovered tools. The chart became the technical preparation for presenting the solution.

The challenge for the management was that the tools were only suitable for rapid prototype development. If management wanted to secure the productivity gains they needed to act quickly to guide the use of these tools and channel the positive results into a more robust data environment.

That proposal lead to a very large and successful effort that reduced the time it took to assemble information to a fraction of the time it took previously. The chart that was used in that first meeting was referenced in numerous meetings afterwards.

When I put that chart together it gave a lot of people a reason

Chapter 5. Where did I leave that chart?

to agree on a single direction that had been tested with available tools. Frankly I did not anticipate the popularity of the ideas communicated in that single chart, but the work that flowed from that first meeting kept me busy for several years to come.

One year later I was asked to present a single graphic chart that could reflect the status of any vehicle tooling program that was stored in the master database. This was a rather challenging task, because it needed to capitalize on the easy to use desktop tools that encouraged the General Motors management to fund a larger project only a year ago. No examples were a part of the request I received nor had anyone within our immediate office or headquarters staff developed any similar applications.

On the other hand that left the final product up to my imagination and ingenuity. This did make it easier to think outside the box in terms of any and all possibilities. An opportunity that I quickly took advantage of by modeling the underlying structure after the prototype that gained great popularity only a year earlier. This early development was the fundamental preparation for the solution yet to come. The creative challenge came when I realized the amount of information that needed to be accessed to support one graphic chart of information.

Regardless of this challenge I was told it would need to be something I worked on after all other scheduling duties. The only way time would be available on a daily basis was if I stayed after hours or took the work home with me. The investment I made in after hours

Chapter 5. Where did I leave that chart?

work seemed minimal when compared to the hours of tedious work the entire office would avoid after a solution was found. As I worked on a vision of what the final product would look like I was encouraged by the incremental progress I made toward the final graphic chart.

After about a month of some rather tedious application programming the first sample chart was ready to be displayed. This new graphic chart that could be generated on a moments notice displayed information present in a dozen pages of text on a single page. This was the technical preparation for the presentation that needed to be complete. Even a manager new to the department could quickly interpret the status of their work on a single graphic chart.

The presentation of the graphic was introduced to upper management by the department manager and met with stunning acceptance. So much so that other departments were asked to present their status in a similar way. These charts were accepted as the standard for reporting information for several years before they were replaced with a somewhat more sophisticated tool for reporting status.

Those three examples were rare instances of successful charts that convinced me how meaningful a single graphic could be when trying to display information and connect with an audience. Here are some lengthy examples that include either video or sound developed by other people that have very powerful messages despite the length of the presentation. Note how these reach for an emotional connection.

- http://www.dow.com/Hu/ (Click on the Hu box)
- http://www.212movie.com

Making Plans to Succeed

W here do people plan to go? The simple answer is a place that requires commitment. Having a vision, setting ambitious goals and developing a workable plan can help sustain people that would otherwise be disappointed and not achieve their goals. Unfortunately, that is not how most people go about the business of achieving goals. It is usually a more haphazard process. If however, the person truly makes a commitment something happens. Making a commitment seems to trigger more resolve and effort even if it does not become a plan. Inspiration may be born out of emotion, but the perspiration it takes to achieve a vision will only be supported by a more logical plan that lays out objectives that lead to accomplished goals. Unfortunately most people are not inspired by plans that expect greater progress with less resources and less time than has been provided in the past. Your vision should consider a comprehensive plan that considers the events, the timing, the commitment, possible changes, the system you work within and the teamwork you will need

Chapter 6. Making Plans to Succeed

as you become responsible for achieving your goals.

Any vision or goal irrespective of size requires some level of commitment. As the level of commitment associated with a goal increases, so to do the number of people pursuing the goal diminish. There are exceptions. If a person has an idealistic vision and has no plan the difficulty achieving that vision requires will be unexpected. As a result, they may be one of many people at the starting line that retreat from that vision after disappointment first occurs. Planning tends to make you aware of the difficulty ahead of time and prepare you for the commitment needed if you are to achieve the goal.

This should not stop those who first dream of achieving a first place finish in a competition. The difference between people and companies that take first place vs. second place is very small and may only be the measure of their emotional ambition to succeed. If you cannot recall the differences between first and second place finishes take moment to visit this web site http://www.212movie.com ; the authors are noted at the end. You may want to take notes. The preceding movie was put together as a motivational tool that seems to stir an emotional ambition within many of us. Despite the emotion you may feel anyone that achieves a first place finish competing with professional competitors will require a plan and emotional energy.

Commitment will require high energy, reevaluation, and constant recovery from disappointment that tends to drain the energy of most people. The preparation for sustaining yourself, should you decide to embark on a journey will depend on the plan you make for

Chapter 6. Making Plans to Succeed

yourself. Plans usually are full of information and will require you to generate questions, process thoughts and take some decisive action as you carry out your plan.

When you think of testing yourself it does not need to start at the base of Mt. Everest. It can be at the dinner table when you describe interesting occurrences of that day. If your family found it interesting or amusing probably a group of your friends would get equal enjoyment from what you had to say. Some stories are told over and over to larger and larger audiences, because they have a common thread that relates to most people. So when you think of taking the first step toward a great adventure just take a small one and enjoy the entire journey every step of the way.

I have encountered many instances of having to take greater risk to reach intermediate goals. Let me walk you through two such experiences. Although the first is not a business related example it does speak to planning and how plans can go wrong when you are reaching for the next level of accomplishment if commitment to fundamentals is not in place. I was in my twenties at the time and feeling like many twenty year olds, indestructible. I got involved in skydiving and was having some difficulty getting off the "static line" and into extended freefall. The static line is a positive parachute opener that takes the decision to open the parachute out of the equation. Until you are off the static line your freefall experience is likely to be limited to several seconds. Likewise the altitude you jump from will typically be limited to something under 3000 feet. Low

Chapter 6. Making Plans to Succeed

altitude jumps were not an exciting experience given the short freefall time available, but how could I break from caution that other licensed and more experienced jumpers recommended?

After discussing the problem that others pinpointed as the stumbling block namely my ability to "get stable" a more senior jumpmaster suggested that if I was willing to go off the static line and go to a higher altitude he would join hands with me and get me stable once and for all. The additional altitude would give me more time to do what I needed to do. Getting stable is very important when it comes to freefall, because if the parachute starts to open and you are not in a stable position, namely spread eagle with your face toward the earth, bad things can happen. Being anxious to get to the next level I quickly agreed and we started to make preparations.

The fly in the soup seemed to be poor communication between me and the jumpmaster. As we discussed what would happen he said, we would jump away from the plane together holding hands. I understood that to mean my holding his right hand with my left hand only. However, he meant my holding his right hand with my left hand and his left hand with my right hand. That small misunderstanding would prove to be rather significant after we exited the plane. With a plane flying at 70 miles per hour or greater and the wind rushing past you at ever increasing speed verbal communication ends once you leave the plane.

Once we reached altitude we both climbed out onto the strut of the airplane. I grasped his right hand with my left hand and when he gave the signal we jumped free of the plane. I tried to get stable without making any effort to grab his other hand and nothing could have been worse. We collided numerous times falling further and further in a rather out of control configuration to say the least.

This did not seem to be working for either of us and at some point the jumpmaster simply pushed me clear and opened his parachute. It was in a split second I realized I needed to get stable and open my parachute. So despite previous failed attempts to accomplish a stable freefall, now I was committed to do what needed to be done or be in greater jeopardy than ever before. This time I got stable even though it contributed to a late parachute opening. Needless to say I never had a problem getting stable again.

This experience underlined the need for greater commitment to the fundamentals. It wasn't simply poor communication, but a lack of commitment to do the fundamental things that were needed to take me to the next level without embarking on what was a very risky strategy to move to the next level of accomplishment.

Some years after my skydiving days a situation developed that demanded I exercise commitment and risk taking to move from a deteriorating financial position. I had been moving from company to company working as a tooling designer when the economy in my geographic area went into a recession. The demand for tooling designers was low enough that newspapers advertisements for tool designers were very sparse and some days nonexistent. I was getting to the bottom of my cash on hand and had to consider my options.

Chapter 6. Making Plans to Succeed

One of my options was to start my own design business on a shoestring. This of all possible options was the riskiest, but it would allow me to avoid relocating to another state where job opportunities were better. So with the last $500 of risk capital I had available I bought the equipment I would need to set up a bare bones office.

As I set out to find a customer it was clear that they were in a pinch to get more done for less. In the first month I had canvassed 50-75 businesses in the metropolitan area with no success. Fortunately the second month yielded a medium size business that needed some design work done quickly and asked me to quote. That was the beginning of a long and prosperous relationship for me.

That first job yielded $2000 payable 30 days after the work was complete. I did work for this company for some seven years and had a great relationship with the owners. At first glance you might say, so what is the big deal? The factor that made this risk acceptable was the plan that limited my risk and prepared me for several months of disappointment that would eventually lead to success.

As a job shop owner you learn very quickly that you are never any better than your last contract, because the demand for your services can drop off overnight. Like all business there are capital expenses, wages and taxes that need to be paid regularly. A business owner that must meet with new customers and sell them on the merits of their product or service is not allowed to share the anxiety that any of the pressure is certain to produce. My negative experience was very minimal compared to business people that have been publicized.

Chapter 6. Making Plans to Succeed

Most business owners I have ever known have been incredible positive thinkers. The successful ones are committed to surviving as a business, and making a profit. These same people recover quickly from disappointment and press forward despite the odds against their succeeding. The most successful are positive and responsible.

One ingredient that needs to be added to any plan is the ability to take responsibility or operate without an instruction book. A plan or a map can be found somewhere based on the travels of someone else, but when things don't go as planned a responsible person needs to say "Here is what we do next." By responsible person I mean someone that doesn't take themselves out of the equation. What needs to be done includes them and they will be there to make it happen. Some people think of themselves as responsible by simply monitoring a situation. The distinction between responsible and irresponsible has to be the level of commitment that the person brings to the party. Without a responsible person available the alternatives may include giving up the goal or at the very least putting it on hold.

How does a person learn to be responsible and self sufficient if they are starting from a place of dependence? Start small and reinforce the gains that advance your independence in likewise small ways. Most behavior is learned and most behavior can be changed. Instead of wishing for change to happen, plan to make the change, and take small steps everyday that fit the plan. When things do not go as planned consider the least steps that need to be taken to get back on track. If the plan is too aggressive and needs to be amended to allow

Chapter 6. Making Plans to Succeed

for greater success then change the plan.

Learning to live without someone telling you what you need to do next to make a success of your life can be learned at any point in your life. The first thing that the dependent person realizes is that independence can be lonely, because if you reject direction from other people they may not understand your need to be independent. The easiest way to orient your friends and business partners to your new independence is to make the decisions they least like to help you make first. It will let them know that you still appreciate their support, but are going to relieve them of a burden they didn't want without saying a thing about it.

Your action will be the best way of communicating your new direction. Be aware that some people may enjoy your dependence on them to make decisions, so they may criticize your new found independence. Address their inquiries as they occur. Thank them for their concern, but let them know that you need to make this decision. Try to avoid a long discussion about your ability to make decisions; just ask for friends to support your independence.

Let's consider plans that can help you achieve a vision. First consider the goals, are the goals likely to change things measurably? Will achieving the goals improve personal or business fortunes significantly? Less ambitious goals may be worth pursuing, but they may not improve either personal or business competitiveness. Accomplished people want to be more competitive. Most people want to be on a par with those who are competitive. One element of being more competitive is achieving significant goals on a regular basis. If the goals do not seek significant committment they are not ambitious. Maybe the goal is a small incremental measurement, but if it is the difference between placing first or second in a widely publicized competition the level of commitment needed is apt to be great.

Judge what is significant with observable and measurable terms. Is the goal coveted by many people? Does the goal seek a 10% improvement in sales? Does the goal seek a 30% improvement in productivity? Is the goal one that is observable and measurable when it is achieved? Is a 5% or 10% improvement in sales easily accomplished? Question, question and question again, goals are the place where all achievement begins.

Just to be clear, my experience at planning is limited and should be considered that of a fly on the wall in the planning room where professional planners rant and rave the virtues of "planning by the book." I have succeeded at planning and accomplishing many personal goals, but that is far different from the lofty criteria of the "Professional Project Planner". Professional planners usually have a long list of credentials and struggle to get organizations to comply with the complexity of their plan requirements. That's not a bad thing it is just the nature of the relationship between operations managers and project planners as I see it from my perspective.

Ambitious goals carry risk, but detailed plans can mitigate risk to a minimum. Planning can be a grueling task or it can be done in a way that matches the need for planning. It is reasonable to say that

Chapter 6. Making Plans to Succeed

one plan or one model for detail does not serve all plans well. Plans like the goals they serve need to be relevant and appropriate while still ambitious in their approach and their application.

The benefits of detailed complicated plans need to be balanced against the available resources and overall benefit. If you consume 75% of all resources with planning you may have ruled out any cost benefit. Many planners in recent days have been lead to believe you can never get too much of a good thing. My approach would say that plans that achieve goals on time and under budget are effective plans, and are the only type of plans to use as reference and models for new plans.

- Plans need to inform
- Objectives should be measurable
- Feedback should forecast plan progress
- Change management should limit change
- Planning should not consume endless resources

Is that ambitions? Some would say it is to simplistic. Many planners have no hesitation to consume limited resources for planning regardless of the percentage of the project it represents.

Once fundamentals of planning are considered you are now ready to consider the timeline of the plan. Is the timeline ambitions? What drives the timeline? Do unrealistic estimates of tasks extend or shorten timing that is driving your timeline? Using unrealistic estimates to press for tighter timelines on planning is slightly disconnected. Selecting these arbitrary early dates ensures an

Chapter 6. Making Plans to Succeed

abnormal rate of failure of the plan and makes progress reports rather worthless. Timelines should be realistic with ambitious goals. Plans need to lead to real measurable incremental changes that build confidence of the project owners.

Plans that continually fail cast doubt on planners as much or more as those responsible for accomplishing the detailed tasks. Planning that reports accurately and realistically seems to be slower and more expensive approach, but it tends to lock in improvement and pay for future change. This type of planning may change the goals that are set, because the emphasis is not on who needs to change, but on what needs to change. If the process you use is too difficult you are likely to waste time discussing the process when you could be measuring progress and reporting improvement.

Many large project plans tend to be obsolete by the time the plans are complete. What is worse is the reluctance to change the planning process regardless of the planning failures. Project planning is most valuable when it meets the need for a plan by those people doing the work.

The goal for changes should include a drive to implement changes that positively impact financial statements quarterly. The financial health of an individual or organization is important to their survival and prosperity over time. Plans for changes that improve financial health are more likely to gain approval. These same plans are more likely to get applause when they succeed.

Simple and complicated project plans need to give proportional

Chapter 6. Making Plans to Succeed

consideration to change management. Although avoiding change may seem to be the best approach some changes should not be ignored.

- Are the changes incremental or revolutionary?
- What is the financial impact of the change?

Improvement can wait, but changes that avoid catastrophic failure are best done as soon as possible. Delays caused by implementing change can be expensive if you consider the impact on sales that need to be made of finished products. Staying on time and under budget may be required to realize financial goals of any one project.

- How do you manage change?
- Are all changes reviewed?
- What is the risk associated with the change?

Early consideration of how requests for change are managed is reasonable, but do not need to be elaborate. Changes may be very worthwhile and cannot be dismissed without consideration. They may even shorten the timeline to completion. Some risk makes the plan ambitious, but unreasonable risk may jeopardize incremental gains needed to repay any capital expenditure.

Be ambitious when setting goals and making plans, but be realistic when evaluating change and managing risk. Successful attempts to make meaningful change do not need to be 100% certain, but when changes contribute financially they are more likely to be accepted. Home run hitters in baseball may have struck out many times; when they connect the potential is great. Conversely when a person wins a spelling bee the individual words may not always seem

Chapter 6. Making Plans to Succeed

difficult, but the winner has no latitude for error. Most successful companies and people do not approach success with the idea that they will succeed 100% of the time. They usually recognize that building a reputation for some single product or effort to be superior will mark the company or individual as successful and a worthy producer. The margin for error is small, but still exists.

A question that should not be overlooked when pursuing difficult to achieve results is do they support a system the company or individual depends on? Improvement that does not support a larger system probably degrades a system by sub-optimizing that same system. System thinking is a safety valve that vents less valued changes. Some changes in early consideration seem exciting and worth pursuing, but after matching it up to "The System" they are exposed as a change that has low value. Many systems need improvement, but moving from one broken system to another is a zero sum gain. If changes are truly worthy they must include those components that address the system they work within. Many times the early analysis uncovers the system connection. Analysis can assist resolving previously missed connections that have far reaching implications.

I always had respect for systems thinking, but was thoroughly convinced of its impact on products and services after I read several books by Eli Goldratt. I first heard of Eli Goldratt while working at General Motors, he was contracted to present his theory in a classroom setting. He called his theory "Theory of Constraints." Not having attended the class but just hearing about it I began to inquire as to the

Chapter 6. Making Plans to Succeed

purpose behind his theory. One manager described it to me as an approach to systems thinking that was easy to understand and was documented in his book "The Goal." The manager said he had received a copy of the book while attending the class and I was free to borrow it if I was interested. I said, sure and he went to his office and retrieved it for me.

That night I began to read it and because of the way it had been written, in a novel format, I stayed up late reading it. The next day I had to buy a copy, because I had so many flags associated with points referenced it seemed like a good idea to get a copy of my own. A couple of days later I returned the book and told the manager how interesting I found the book.

Larry said, "Well you know he wrote another book called "Critical Chain" that explores that theory relative to planning and scheduling. As it just so happens I have that book on my desk. I haven't read it yet, but if you are interested I would be glad to let you borrow that book." I could not resist and took the second book, thinking all along nothing could have been as good as that first book.

That night I began to read the first few pages of the second book. I was hooked, again the approach the author used had me marking pages only to be interrupted by dinner and restroom breaks. It was a fascinating approach to systems thinking that didn't put me to sleep while I read the book. I then decided to look up Eli Goldratt to find out more about the man. As I searched his web site I noticed he listed three books as companion pieces, "The Goal, Critical Chain and

Chapter 6. Making Plans to Succeed

It's Not Just Luck." You guessed it I had to buy the both the second and the third books.

A few weeks later I was discussing what I had read with a neighbor and Carolyn said, "You know Eli will be in town all next week giving a seminar in Warren, Michigan." I couldn't help myself I had to meet the man that had provided me with so many hours of information and entertainment. The next week I made a trip to the seminar unannounced and carrying all three books.

Eli Goldratt did not appear to be leading the seminar so when the presenters took a break I introduced myself and explained my reason for coming. His children who were the presenters said, "Wait here a moment." They came back and said Eli would like to meet you and autograph your books. For the next hour I sat with Eli Goldratt discussing the impact his work was having on General Motors and how it impacted my life. We discussed his "Theory of Constraints" and how helpful it was from the office floor to the production room in an effort to inform people of the importance of system thinking. I was sold on systems thinking after that day, and with no regrets.

Even when people give consideration to the system that may have greater influence on the outcome of changes or improvements, the leadership that is required will include overcoming some fear of failure. As a leader the individual is subject to self doubt. Fearing failure will influence people that plan both personal and business goals. As Winston Churchill said "Success is going from failure to failure without loss of enthusiasm". It is not a matter of

Chapter 6. Making Plans to Succeed

ignoring failure, but one of learning from it sufficient to succeed. Plenty of books have been written about how people have succeeded after confronting real world problems that plague personal success and business success. Probably the one that stands out in my reading is a book by Lance Armstrong and Sally Jenkins entitled "It's Not About the Bike: My Journey Back to Life". For people that haven't had their life interrupted by life threatening illness it should be inspiring.

So by way of review, ambitious ideas that have immediate value consider the systems they are intended to improve or replace. More specifically, ambitious ideas that people are apt to pay for should include some formal planning that seeks the owner's approval on a regular basis. You may not be reminded of Thomas Edison and his accomplishments or Madame Currie and her best moments, so what is missing? The answer is risk. Greater risk will lead to greater accomplishment but less frequently. Now with that in mind it needs to be mentioned that most people and businesses are opposed to high risk, but many people and businesses have learned to allot a portion of their resources to high risk projects. Individuals may look at these efforts as an investment in growth and development, while companies routinely refer to high risk projects as research. Research efforts are infrequently publicized unless they achieve notable results. The successes are reviewed publicly in hopes of justifying the total research effort.

Look for examples of "research effort" in the lives of individuals and companies. Without the success that is accomplished we would never have known the extent of the effort that went into the success. Who is aware of the hours of work that goes into the conditioning of an athlete unless they become well known? How many athletes put in long hours of training and never share the spotlight of those that are successful? How many companies and people within those companies' labor long hours without notice unless their company is identified as having achieved some significant goal as compared to all other companies? Successful people and companies accept risk as a part of life and manage the risk while doing the routine tasks that allow them to grow and prosper in smaller increments. Including some high risk investments, even on a limited basis, is a perspective that most successful people and businesses embrace. If you agree with the previously mentioned approach you may be wondering, where do I start if I haven't already?

Start reaching for the success that is most immediate to your own life. Don't try to imitate someone else. Become aware of what is of interest to you and seek mastery and accomplishment in these areas first and foremost. All success has a way of encouraging continued success and long term great success. Patience and persistence coupled with some tolerance for risk is likely to give you a winning perspective as you succeed from day to day at routine tasks.

Developing a perspective is important if you hope to establish a relatively independent life. You need to be able to look back over days, months and years to reinforce the progress you make away from being dependant. Taking responsibilities for both small and big

Chapter 6. Making Plans to Succeed

decisions as you work your way from one event to another will be necessary. Consulting others about the alternatives is always valid, so try to add some piece of your consideration to make the direction one you can say that you own. Without owning the decision you can always slip out from accepting the responsibility.

If you ever expect to go where you plan to go, you will need to be prepared to think for yourself on a regular basis. If until now you have only been a spectator, consider that achievement based on your ability to unlock the value of information is not a spectator sport. It requires your involvement. Create a plan that supports your vision and if you are a dependent person consider what you need to do to gain more independence.

Some people that have slowly become dependent on others to direct their action do not realize how devastating losing that support could be if only by accident. It is wise for any person adventurous or not to nurture greater independence if only to carry them through periods when outside assistance is not readily available. Your goals may be modest, but unlocking the value of information will be needed unexpectedly.

How does independence impact teamwork? Today many workforces encourage teamwork and even insist on it. Independent thinking has a place in teamwork. When teams need new ideas to advance their effort they will do "Brainstorming" to identify new and perhaps independent thinking. If you have a new idea you need to be prepared to explore with others how it could make a positive difference.

Teams will always need leadership and here again an independent thinker has an opportunity to contribute to the team. Leadership requires energy and initiative that you can contribute. When the team does not work as a team the leader must reestablish the rhythm that a team needs to be more effective than the sum of its parts. A leader needs to motivate others to succeed by example. Demonstrating how success is accomplished even in a small way can encourage others to contribute to a larger effort.

Teamwork and teams in general are recognized as being more capable than most individuals. They are typically made up of many capable people and the best teams learn to use the individual talents of each person to complement the performance of the team. The accomplishments of teams are generally more significant than that of individuals. Teams climb mountains, sail the ocean, cross the desert or just play for top honors in an arena. Many very talented individuals find that joining a team is the only way they can achieve certain goals.

Businesses recognize this and given the coordination needed to be an effective business they find teamwork an asset to the way they do business. Some of the businesses that are driving hardest to achieve success depend on strong individuals to lead teams that are expected to produce results that take the company where plans suggest. The responsible individual is more important than ever as companies rely on teams and teamwork to produce results.

Just as business depends on teamwork so does the family.

Chapter 6. Making Plans to Succeed

Who is the team leader in your family? Does anyone share the leadership duties? How does your family team support your goals? Is teamwork discussed? Some families are run like some businesses. That may mean that the family operates more like a benevolent dictatorship than it does like a team. That is because teamwork is very deliberate and takes a great deal of time and effort to achieve.

What is your situation? Where do you want to go? Will it take some planning? Do you have a plan? Is it ambitious or easy to achieve? Do you feel challenged by your circumstances or do you live a blessed life? Asking yourself these questions give you a chance to evaluate where you stand. Are you on a path of achievement today as compared to the past? Developing a perspective on today helps consider where you have been and where you are going.

If you have a plan for the future, review it frequently. Keeping your plans for the future current will help support the small efforts you need to take everyday to achieve a higher ground tomorrow. As you achieve the markers you have set for yourself don't forget to celebrate your achievement. Some people insist that plans need to be on paper. If you tend to achieve your goals routinely without a paper plan don't feel compelled to clutter your desk with more paper. However, if your plans seem to slip and are infrequently correct write it down and carry your plan around in your pocket as a reminder.

Your effort needs to center around results. Do what you need to do to achieve results everyday. Small accomplishments have a way of accumulating into a significant result.

CHAPTER 7

Accomplishment and Perspective

Accomplishment may be something that comes more easily to some people than to others. If being accomplished is one of those things that does not come easily to you try to review the following points and consider where you stand on a scale from a 1-10. To be perceived by others as accomplished you should be scoring eight or higher.

- High Energy
- Focus
- Patience and Persistence
- Analysis without Paralysis
- Open to Outside Opinions
- Acts Decisively

Don't be discouraged if you are strong on some points and weak on others, because that is the most likely situation. Strive to include all points in your approach. You may need to balance what you lack in one area with the effort you make in another area. You may need to

Chapter 7. Accomplishment and Perspective

add a coach or mentor to your plan. The experience of others is valued information that may save you many steps on your way to accomplishing your goals.

Energy and effort are among the first considerations. Using information will always require effort, because how information will be used has infinite possibilities. Sifting through mounds of information to distill clear thoughts for your perspective will be required. As you consider your energy level give some thought as to your source of energy. What makes you feel energized? Some people attribute their energy to a spiritual source, while others might say it is simply being physically fit. Whatever the answer is for you it deserves consideration, because there will be times when you feel exhausted at a time when stopping to rest is not an option.

If you take time during periods of rest to think through your source of energy it will be easier to maintain or energize yourself on a regular basis. Once you have identified sources of energy taking action to replenish your energy level daily should be a routine that sustains you. Patiently coach yourself to make time in every day to do what renews your energy level and enables you to persist in the face of adversity. If the goal is one hour a day start small and set aside 15 minutes a day. Once you have achieved 15 minutes celebrate and move to the next incremental marker until you have met your goal. If somewhere along the way one hour is not the right number back off to 45 minutes. The point is you need to think about what gives you strength and energy and make time for it everyday.

Chapter 7. Accomplishment and Perspective

People that maintain high energy levels are more likely to persist in their purpose when other people will step aside to rest. Expending extra effort as you strive to achieve even modest goals is good practice for those times that test your resolve and capacity to keep going. Although you can get too much of a good thing, having an ability to reach inside yourself for the energy you need in times of stress and challenge can be a good thing.

A couple of experiences while I was young demonstrated for me how digging deep for that reserve energy can either help make seemly extraordinary efforts seem rather ordinary or make the same efforts rather dangerous. Knowing the difference may be the lesson learned only after things go wrong.

When I was 15 years old I was accustomed to riding my bike for fairly long distances during the summer. Occasionally I would travel from the outskirts of Detroit where I lived to Belle Isle to go swimming in the Detroit River. This was approximately a 20 mile round trip all things considered. One Saturday morning I got up and announced to my mother "I think I'll take a bike ride to Island Lake", this was about a 40 mile trip one way. Although she just said to me on my way out the door "OK", she later told me she thought to her self that "Oh he will turn around and come back after about an hour."

Well after the first hour I had covered about ten miles or so and because it was such a beautiful day I just kept going. There were several times when going back was a consideration due to the hills that were a part of the route. Some hills had me walking on the gravel at

Chapter 7. Accomplishment and Perspective

the side of the road and thinking this might not have been such a good idea. Great memories of having visited the Island Lake area around Brighton, Michigan many times before with my family kept me going. I didn't reach Island Lake until around one o'clock in the afternoon. That was about a five hour ride. Meaning to leave for home at about four o'clock I went to the State Park and went swimming. Then I stopped off at the arcade and played a few games and finally had a bite to eat at the outdoor hotdog stand. It had gotten dark and was close to ten o'clock when it finally occurred to me that I needed to leave.

Not wanting my mother to worry about me I called home and told her I would be a little late. Well needless to say she wasn't the least bit comforted by the idea that I would be traveling at night on a two lane highway for the next five hours. She insisted I stay right where I was and she had my sister come pick me up. As luck would have it my sister had other plans, but figured this was a priority. My sister wasn't too upset that she had to change her plans after all it was her brother. Looking back on that it seemed remarkable that I even found the energy to make the trip one way let alone propose that I would make my way home after a rather active day.

That experience certainly made me more cautious going forward, but what happens when two people exercise poor judgment and one of them is your father? How could he have known? Even now as I recall this incident it seems that many people even today are not aware of the risk that this next activity brings with it.

When I was 16 years old I found out how reaching deep and

calling on every source of energy can sometimes take an unexpected bad turn. It was a sunny warm Saturday and my father who was visiting my aunt called me up at home and asked if I was interested in going swimming at my aunts' swimming pool. Of course the answer was yes, but I didn't know then what a memorable day that would be as I reflect back on it now at age 62.

My father and I had been engaged in scuba diving and even some free diving, or diving without an aqua lung for about a year at this time. We had reviewed the record books for some of the times that free divers in the South Seas had achieved underwater. We spent many hours swimming and extending our times underwater comparing notes on how we accomplished our goals.

Well this Saturday we continued our quest for a new marker. The pool was a large pool, approximately 50 foot long by 25 feet wide. We never discussed what might go wrong and if it did what we would do about it. We were always having too much fun to do that kind of preparation. My father stated, "I will make it around the perimeter of the pool twice without surfacing." Of course with my aunt and uncle looking on I wasn't going to be outdone. I said, "If you can make it around twice I will make it three times."

The method we had used to succeed in the past was about to be the method that made things really dangerous. Over the months we had conditioned ourselves to stay underwater for extended periods. We learned to ignore the warning signs that your body uses to tell you that you have gone too far. When my father went to the bottom of the pool

Chapter 7. Accomplishment and Perspective

and worked his way around I could see that he was in extreme stress and expected him to give up somewhere short of the two laps. My father was a smoker and in the past it usually limited his distance underwater. Today that wasn't the case and after two laps underwater he came to the surface like a great whale gasping for breath.

Well the game was on and now it was my turn to do everything I could to beat his accomplishment by half. As I prepared he said how difficult his effort was as compared to other times. I thought he was just trying to talk me out of it, so I made my preparations not knowing what was ahead. The water was warm the sun was out and I didn't have a care in the world.

As I submerged for my trip around the perimeter it occurred to me that this shouldn't be that difficult given we had the entire pool to ourselves and the water was calm and undisturbed. After the first lap I still felt strong and concentrated on swimming efficiently to conserve my oxygen from the gulps of air I had taken so long ago. Passing the second lap gave me additional energy knowing I had past the mark my father had set, but I still had a full lap to go.

We had started out in the shallow end of the pool, so as I closed in on two and a half laps I followed the pool to the deep end. Just as I swam across the deep end of the pool everything went black. We never anticipated that either one of us could blackout from such behavior, but there I was at the bottom of a ten foot pool blacked out. My father immediately jumped in to rescue me yelling for help as he jumped in to pull me up. My aunt and uncle thought he was kidding at first, but when they saw my somewhat blue body being pulled up on the side of the pool they came to my fathers' aid.

It wasn't until my father had me on the deck, flat on my face and pressed on my back to expel the water that I awoke to three people standing over me. As I coughed up the water and regained my normal color my father asked what had happened. All I could recall was my position in the pool at the deep end. We had both learned a lesson that day that has remained with me to this day, and that is you need to set reasonable limits on your expected achievement. That experience frightened us to the extent that we never competed in that way again.

If high energy were the only consideration, most people do not have the energy level that is necessary to propel them to significant accomplishment. Many people with only ordinary energy levels and even diminished energy levels have succeeded against great odds. The ability to concentrate sufficient energy seems to be related to a person's ability to focus on the task at hand and persist from task to task until they reach the intended objective. Focus is a way that any person can do more with less. Focus minimizes the effort needed to accomplish tasks, because it discards those things that would distract the individual and drain whatever energy they have available.

Some athletes refer to this ability to focus as "getting into the zone". Most of us can recall some outstanding athletic performance, where the athlete seems to be focused and performing on an exceptional basis. What about everyday on the job performance? Are there times you can "get in the zone" in a work environment? The answer is a resounding yes. As a designer I would routinely get into a well focused state of mind that tended to block out surrounding interference. This allowed me to work tirelessly for hours without a break in my activity. These focused hours would allow me to turn out work in a fraction of the time other less focused designers could produce.

While working for a company that had many designers I found how striking the difference could be when working side by side. I was hired to design one piece of equipment that was a part of a multiple set. I had been brought in after the other designers had been working on their individual pieces for about a week. I was expected to complete the contract in approximately four or more weeks.

Contract designers, working on a predefined price, are extremely competitive while designers that simply work by the hour do not seem to have that same competitive nature. I was a contract designer in a sea of hourly designers. This did not change how I approached the work, because I knew the price for my work was already agreed to ahead of starting any work at all. The first few days I spent getting focused on what exactly needed to be done.

At first this raised questions with the management that was accustom to watching designers work in a manner that I would refer to as "thinking on paper". The designers would put all their thoughts on paper including the wrong ones. As they would discover the error they would change it, but the process was extremely time consuming. However from the management perspective they were busy doing

Chapter 7. Accomplishment and Perspective

what they needed to do. Management was concerned I would not complete my piece of the work until well after all other pieces of equipment had been designed. I reassured them that wouldn't happen and they kept their distance as I gathered my thoughts.

After the first day or two I started to draw the design for the piece of equipment with only minor revisions. At the end of three weeks my piece of equipment was complete and designs of all the others were still in some stage of completion. The management asked me to stay on for another assignment, but it was clear to me that my fellow designers were not happy with my presence. After that I tended to work alone out of my own office content with my performance and available contracts. That level of focus enabled me to price my work very competitively from that point on.

Not enough can be said for patience with oneself and persistence of purpose. Persistent beavers create large homes; persistence ants create enormous ant hills as they work together. Accomplishments of people will employ a higher ordered thought process and allow people to complement persistence with patience.

Perhaps people tend to lose their advantage by resorting to over analysis that paralyzes their ability to act. Deciding to act has consequences but likewise avoidance of action is not likely to ever achieve much of anything. Action must be guided by information that gives us the best possible chance at success, but there are no sure bets. Analysis must be followed by a decision making process that evaluates the best possible direction.

Chapter 7. Accomplishment and Perspective

Consideration and analysis are important to avoiding wasted effort, but equally important is the decision to act. Accomplished people are able to decide and act. Persistent action that achieves limited objectives leads the least of us to achieve great goals over time. A sense of where we start and where we are relative to greater goals is perspective that can be a part of analysis that sustains our effort to achieve success.

Much is written about analysis of goals, the plans and objectives to achieve success but not much is written about perspective. Perspective or point of view can be an encouragement or discouragement. The way to draw energy and encouragement from perspective is to adjust the focus. When you look backward achievement is easy to spot and drawing encouragement from past success is not a difficult task. Looking forward usually tends to focus us on the most difficult of tasks yet to be accomplished and trigger some level of discouragement. If we shift our focus to the mechanics of achieving a task, much in the same way the beaver or the ant focus on the sliver of wood or the grain of sand and keep moving forward, we would find that patience and persistence is of greater value than brute strength in accomplishing our goals. Breaking down the future into bite size tasks helps secure much more historical success. We can then draw encouragement to deal with the unknown difficulty that lies ahead, because it is not as difficult as we first thought.

When you keep moving forward not only do you tend to get more done you improve your perspective, because every time you look up you are further ahead. Nothing is more discouraging than to see no progress unless it is to see lost effort derived from set backs. No progress and lost ground are only significant if steady progress isn't made on a daily basis. Keep moving and keep acting on the objectives in front of you and progress in most instances is inevitable.

I was not immune from the struggle to keep moving and achieving objectives. As a team member I agreed to a plan that had required each of us to contribute significantly at different points in the development process. The difficulty with my contribution was that it covered a significant portion of uncharted water. Some of what was needed had not been accomplished in the past. A further complication was that there was no instruction book or resident expert available for consultation. The development was theoretically plausible but no method for getting the results had been established.

This development team that was putting together computer programs for training people at the Chrysler Corporation consisted of several department members. Jack and Bob were my immediate teammates that handled artistic elements, pedagogy and general programming portions of the project. They needed to do the bulk of the development that preceded my contribution. Their contribution was as worthy as anything I would contribute, but I can only give you a perspective on my struggle to persevere.

The day they informed me they had completed their portions of the development left me several days to knit together their components along with the existing portions of the system that had been

Chapter 7. Accomplishment and Perspective

established in earlier programming efforts. Prior to this event I had worked out several scenarios that could possibly lead to successful completion of the programming.

I found out rather quickly that many of those options worked in limited ways but were insufficient when it came to this new configuration. As the hours pasted I exhausted more and more options if only by trial and error. It was clear to me the original solutions I had considered were not working after the first 24 hours of non-stop programming.

Jack and Bob were both concerned as our deadline drew near, but I assured them it was just a bump in the road. On the inside my stomach was churning and I wasn't quite sure what I needed to do next. I continued on for another 12 hours finding some part of the solution along the way. Once a workable solution emerged it became obvious the only thing between where I was and finishing the work was a mountain of tedious coding. We had set a deadline that was now only two days away. I spent approximately another fifteen hours finishing the package that would be replicated and delivered to 100 machines at a dozen or so locations.

After more than two days of non-stop programming my brain was scrambled, it left Jack and Bob a short time to make duplicates for final distribution. I had been without answers any number of times as I pushed through the trial and error solutions that were left, but at some level it seemed like patience and persistence would be the ultimate decider of when the answer would arrive. We succeeded as a team for that first launch and I am sure that I wasn't the only person that struggled to get a piece of the work done. It was a moment that for me tested my patience and persistence of purpose.

Clear thinking may reveal negative aspects of an issue but high achievers seek a perspective that mitigates the negative and accentuates the positive. This may pose something less than a realistic perspective, but the reality of others does not threaten the high achiever. High achievers may clearly see reality but work to create a new reality acting decisively not paralyzed by the conflict that any analysis may bring.

One day while still in my twenties I was sitting and watching a world wide ski jumping competition on a 90 meter ski jump. It occurred to me that the ski jumpers were using a technique that I had been using in freefall as a skydiver. They would keep their hands to their side and with ever so slight hand movements change their direction through the air. Having the experience of 50-60 skydives I felt confident that if I could just learn to ride the slide I could probably ski jump.

Without much concern for the fact that I had not skied since I was about 10 years old at my cousins house on a hill, which translates to virtually no skiing experience to my credit the search for a ski jumping resort began that day. The first location identified was a small out of the way lodge near Cadillac, Michigan. Without any hesitation I made a trip up there the very next weekend. Briar Hill was a small out of the way lodge that had just what I was looking for in a

Chapter 7. Accomplishment and Perspective

place to start a new adventure.

First I got to know some of the people and was introduced to a seasoned ski jumper by the name of Adolf. He held the record jump for the 50 meter hill. I told him of my interest to ski jump that was born out of my sky diving experience which he found odd but interesting. He said before I would be allowed on the ski jumping hill I would need to learn to ski the bunny hill, the intermediate slope and the advanced slope with moguls.

He said all you need to do is make three passes on each and he would coach me on the ski jump hill. Without hesitation I started to meet the markers Adolf had set. By the end of the second week and the forth day of skiing I was making my final three passes down the advanced hill. It wasn't pretty as a matter of fact the few people on the hill knew to give me a wide space to make my pass. That evening I was allowed to ride the landing of the 30 meter ski jump. I think they gave me that permission just to get me out of the way of the other skiers.

When I returned the third week I was full of hope that I could ride the ski jump. With some additional practice riding the landing I was allowed onto the 30 meter jump. My first jump was not anything to write home about, but it was my first. In my opinion things could only get better given that first jump. As I made run after run things did get better and later that day Adolf assured me that tomorrow I would ride the 50 meter jump.

A storm came in that night and made me postpone my date

with the 50 meter jump until the following weekend. The next week I was out on the slope early packing the landing with great anticipation of what the day would hold. When Adolf arrived we went to the ski jump hill and Adolf said, "Before going on the 50 meter jump he would like to see me make a few good passes on the 30 meter jump again."

Without hesitation I went up and made my first pass. It could only be described as bad. I lost something between last week and this and just about ended the week before it got started. After numerous runs with one no better than the last Adolf said, "I will be down in the lodge if you find out what went wrong let me know."

Disappointed but not discouraged I began to analyze what was wrong. After several rides on the landing ramp it occurred to me what was going wrong. I had unintentionally narrowed my focus to the slope directly in front of me. This didn't allow for an orientation to the trees that were in my peripheral vision. As a result I was pitching either too far forward or too far backward after leaving the jump making the landing dangerous. I had come close to nose diving into the landing almost as many times as I came close to landing on by back. After making adjustments to my focus I made a few perfect runs on the 30 meter to test the theory then headed for the lodge to tell Adolf.

Adolf was hesitant to believe the problem was remedied until he returned and saw for himself that each pass down the ramp was better than the last. That afternoon I climbed to the top of the 50 meter slide. Two younger boys were up at the top and said they would wait until I made my jump. I thanked them but told them to go ahead of me, because I would need some time to prepare for that first jump on the 50 meter slide.

The slide was a rough lumber structure that was approximately thirty to fifty feet above the landing that dropped several hundred feet back toward the lodge. As I stood there for a few minutes I noticed something odd. The people on the adjacent slope where I had made a few blazing down hill runs that bordered on being out of control obviously were informed that something special was about to happen, because as I stood there they all were motionless and looking back as if to say, "Oh No." Not intending any pressure just some level of disbelief that the same person they saw crash and burn more than once was perched above the trees about to challenge common wisdom.

I lined up my skis and got in position and pushed off. Unfortunately my right ski pivoted over my left just as I started down the slide and an emergency was underway. In a split second I lifted my right foot and placed it in the proper groove and just in time to stand up and fly off the end of the slide toward the landing. The landing had a flat spot from the end of the slide to the ramp about 10 meters out, because I only stood up at the end and didn't thrust myself forward I hit the last few feet of the flat spot that launched me once again further down the landing ramp.

When I got to the bottom I was elated that all the troubleshooting on the way down seemed to work out. When I got back up to the top of the hill Adolf said, "It was a little bit like watching a cat find its footing as it fell from a tree." Despite the criticism I persisted the rest of the day improving on every jump. The lesson here is that a vision that no one else shared came to pass despite set backs. Analysis did not lead to paralysis, but instead decisive action was followed by success.

Seeking positive outcomes will certainly shape perspective, but it does not prevent observing situations objectively. Positive thinkers far and wide insist that individuals and organizations can create their own reality. Does this prevent clear thinking? No, it simply promotes positive thinking. Positive thinkers may not know how some difficulty will be resolved instead they just keep on planning to succeed against all odds.

Can you think of instances in your own life when your experience included high energy, focus, patience, persistence, analysis without paralysis, outside influence, and decisive action? They don't need to be extreme to either be meaningful or memorable. Although the times that all of these elements come together may be rare, they should help inform you of your capacity to think clearly with some perspective that sustains continuing efforts to succeed in so many different ways.

Many people discount their individual efforts as less than significant, but any effort to succeed at a higher level is preceded by less than significant performance. It is the continued and almost compulsive need to succeed that finally yields a performance that stands out from all other performances.

Any of the instances where you have succeeded were probably preceded by some disappointment. Sometimes patience and persistence is not enough, you may need to find more energy or take decisive action to move to the next level. Each experience needs to be evaluated separately. As you analyze what is needed don't fall into the trap of analysis that paralyzes you. If there are several possible known improvements that may help just pick one and evaluate the results after you implement the change.

When the experience is yours and you recognize who owns the process you may be less objective. Reviewing the life experience of someone else after it occurs provides a perspective not easily achieved as an individual struggling toward a goal in the heat of the moment. Coaches and mentors contribute insight that may seem harsh at the moment, but when observed by the spectator it was an intervention that was needed to improve direction. Coaches are a great way to make subtle changes that contribute greatly to your performance.

Consider outside coaching or mentoring if only as a temporary measure to help you establish an improved performance. Many people including professionals don't hesitate to get help, because they know that their fortunes hang in the balance. Failure or just consistent bad performance is not an option for these people. As you consider coaching or mentoring consider what top competitor avoids coaching or mentoring? Few accomplished performers avoid coaching of any form. This includes business people as well as the more obvious sports figures.

Companies that are noted for having visible mentors that have nurtured both the company and the people to high performance would include General Electric and General Motors. Jack Welch became an example that others have followed at General Electric. He not only mentored people that would succeed him, but he nurtured a system that could nurture others for years after he was gone. At General Motors Bob Lutz restructured the process that has provided award winning automobile designs and a system that will be there for years to come long after he leaves the company.

Coaching and mentoring has become an industry on to itself for a wide variety of individuals and businesses alike. The categories address individual improvement to specific job skills that can help sports figures and businesses achieve goals. The guidance coaching and mentoring provides, improves the performance of some people greatly in relatively short periods of time.

CHAPTER 8

Learning Without Making Fatal Mistakes

Learning anything usually risks failure at some level. Taking risk is a very personal activity. Some people have a low tolerance for risk and consider they are a failure if they have lost ten percent of their investment. Other people have lost their fortune along with the fortune of many others and persist until they accumulate wealth and understanding that prevents a repeat of past errors. There are also those people that have no fear and persist to loose big until they finally make a fatal error. Fatal errors are those that cost you your health, put you on the wrong side of the law, and at a minimum cost you family and business relationships that have been a stabilizing force in your life. Certainly there are some extreme examples of people reclaiming their lives despite jail time and divorce, but ambition to succeed does not require extreme levels of risk. Sometimes the only way fatal errors can be avoided is by coping with events as they occur. Developing coping skills from an information perspective means unlocking value in real-time.

Chapter 8. Learning Without Making Fatal Mistakes

Rapid success is related to striking a meaningful connection with potential customers not taking unreasonable risk. Risk will always be part of learning to succeed, but do not be sold on the value of unreasonable risk. High risk is probably more closely related to faulty thinking and limited information than it is to great opportunity. When a person offers what seems like a great opportunity coupled with extreme risk, ask others that are not involved for their perspective on the offer.

Many questionable products or services that promise quick profits depend on the greed of the potential customer. Unbridled greed or gambling are conditions more likely associated with illness or a character flaw than they are someone destined to succeed. Following good business models for making a reasonable profit are more apt to lead to success over time. Evaluating risk depends on sufficient information analysis that clearly identifies what is needed to reduce risk. Investment is usually made with the future in mind so reducing risk going forward is a reasonable position. Avoiding fatal investment errors should be the primary concern not an after thought when investments go badly. Post mortems of disastrous investments usually turn up information that indicated high risk and no connection to good business models. To ignore the need to collect, analyze and evaluate information that we eventually decide to act on makes our actions ineffective at best.

Avoiding fatal mistakes starts with the realization that careful decision making goes a long way in avoiding bad results, but all

Chapter 8. Learning Without Making Fatal Mistakes

learning brings risk. Making mistakes is just an everyday occurrence, but considering ways to avoid making mistakes a part of a product or service is needed to succeed in business. Sometimes you are not even aware of the risk you have been subject to until after the event. You may literally only be along for the ride.

It happened to me at age thirteen when my father thought that my flying lessons should include stalls and spins. Not being advised in advance I wasn't abnormally nervous that Sunday we went to the airport. It was after the instructor took me to the flight equipment shack to get me fitted for a parachute that some concern crept into my mind. As we went to the plane he informed me that we would be doing some stalls and spins as a part of the lesson today.

At age thirteen I was about five foot eight inches and weighed about 160 pounds. The reason I mention it is, because it seemed to escape the notice of the instructor that day. It was not important until sometime later, but it was at that time that it should have been considered. Just to point out some contrast the instructor was about five foot six and about 130 pounds soaking wet.

We were flying a plane that was referred to as a tail dragger. The significance of that was that the plane had two seats one directly behind the other. The student typically was positioned in the forward seat and the instructor sat in back. Well as the lessons began all went well and I was getting the hang of stalling the plane and recovering to a normal flight pattern. The next step was to learn something about spins.

Chapter 8. Learning Without Making Fatal Mistakes

The instructor told me to let him use the tandem controls that were in the back to demonstrate how to enter the spin from a stall and recover. We did that a few times and then he asked that I take the controls and go from the stall into the spin and then recover. As we went into the stall it occurred to me how surreal an experience it all seemed to me. As a pilot you did not have a feeling that you were plummeting toward earth as you headed into the spin, because you were somewhat pressed back in your seat and felt a bit weightless.

We went into the first revolution of the spin and then the second revolution and as we closed in on the third revolution I heard the instructor say, "I think it is time to recover from the spin" in a rather loud voice. It was a rather fascinating experience, but the instructor was quite clear that in the future I should start to pull out of the spin after only one and a half revolutions. Although I enjoyed the three revolution spin experience he seemed a bit abrupt afterwards.

When we got back on the ground I found out why he was a little on edge. As we discussed the experience with my father the instructor said that he had tried to get my attention after the second revolution of the spin. When I didn't quickly acknowledge him he was concerned that he wouldn't able to pull me off the controls all the way to the ground given his size vs. mine. No one was more relieved than he was when I finally acknowledged his second request to pull back on the controls and recover from that rather fascinating spin.

It is funny how perceptions of a situation can vary between two people experiencing the same thing at the same time. The difference

Chapter 8. Learning Without Making Fatal Mistakes

is of course easily explained by the vast difference in the experience level between the two people. No fatal mistakes that day.

One of the things that will always distinguish you from others will be your thought processes. One process that is extremely important is the process you use to achieve quality, because it is understood that even if error is inevitable error ridden products and services are not. Mikel Harry and Richard Schroeder in their book *Six Sigma, The Breakthrough Management Strategy Revolutionizing The World's Top Corporations 2006* give extensive consideration to the subject of quality, but you will need some system less complex to regulate your personal activity.

My personal favorite approaches are described by positive thinkers that have succeeded in spite of failure or adversity. Although I have never personally met them, I find the words of Anthony Robbins and Joel Osteen truly inspiring when you are looking to recover from errors that seem small, but can accumulate and halt your personal growth. I will leave it to you to select from their writings, because what they have written or said is available in many different forms. They are among the best examples of the good that can come from positive thinking.

Positive thinking is an element of persistence. We all need to survive a level of failure that is discouraging yet not fatal. Positive thinking does not and should not ignore reality or give us a warped perspective of the challenges we face. A positive attitude instead recognizes the reality and gives us courage to persist and overcome

Chapter 8. Learning Without Making Fatal Mistakes

extreme odds despite repeated failure. Some people have a positive attitude that is secular in nature and others have a religious basis. The secular side is less familiar to me, but some names from the late 1800's and early 1900's come to mind such as Orison Swett Marden, Emile Coue, Sigmund Freud and Carl Gustav Jung. Although they may not be as familiar as Anthony Robbins and Joel Osteen or Norman Vincent Peale they have had an impact on the history of what we call "Positive Thinking."

If "Positive Thinking" is not something you have as a part of your everyday coping skills it is well worth the time to nurture that element of your persistence. You may be a naturally positive person and scoff at those people that need to exercise that part of the way they view life, but even some of the most positive thinking people can turn negative during a significant event in their life. When positive people go negative they probably would benefit by heeding the words of any one of those positive thinkers I mentioned earlier.

Before you start applying positive thinking to all things take time to understand there are negative behaviors that cannot be overcome by simply thinking positive. When you buy a lottery ticket and it becomes a looser, thinking that "next week I'll be more likely to win" is not positive thinking. Sitting at a slot machine for long periods of time does not ensure the likelihood of the machine repaying you for your losses. Drinking to forget your problems and continuing the practice day after day to avoid a sober life is not positive thinking. Some behaviors are just plain bad decisions that can spiral out of

Chapter 8. Learning Without Making Fatal Mistakes

control and will require some decision on your part along with support from others to correct.

Avoiding all risk to avoid fatal errors restricts learning. Look at learning as an opportunity to gain perspective and share experience. Probably the greatest danger behind unnecessary risks is that they discourage a persistent effort to learn and succeed even if they don't scar you for life. It is important to avoid life altering failure, because it interrupts persistent effort for long periods of time.

If you are unsure if your problems evolve from bad decisions or just a lack of patience, persistence and positive thinking ask a trusted friend or a paid professional. Depending on an outside opinion may be the first step in the right direction for many people that are confused about their lack of success. Many people that are successful may still feel unfulfilled. Using a professional or an old friend to help sort through these feelings is a way to seek the analysis of information that until then was of little value. Other perspectives can be very useful in adding value to information that from your solitary perspective had little meaning. Working with others does not remove you from the decision making process.

Working with others just gives you the advantage of another analysis of the same information you may struggle to understand. The decision to follow one path or another will always belong to you as an individual. Very accomplished people have been known to use the opinions of others to evaluate the decisions they make to achieve lifetime goals. An easily understood example could include some of those people that have tried to climb Mt. Everest. In the past people making this kind of effort were seasoned very self reliant mountain climbers. Today people from all walks of life are going to Mt. Everest with limited climbing experience as compared to some of the people to first climb the mountain. They generally depend on seasoned guides to prepare and lead the trek up the mountain. What some don't seem to understand is that conditions on the mountain can occur that will overwhelm the best of plans and support. When that happens the individual stands alone to decide and perhaps to guide themselves from a dangerous precipice to a place of safety. The decision that the individual makes in these instances may be the difference between life and death. Regardless of the best opinions and direction the individual must still take responsibility for themselves.

Preparing yourself for significant negative events ahead of time by learning something about positive thinking may help avoid spiraling out of control when a tragedy occurs. Your normal responses may get you through anything, but being prepared only gives you more options. It does not matter if you prefer the secular approach over the religious approach just be prepared, because most significant negative events are unpredictable.

If you need a good example of someone that made a "fatal error" and struggled to recover some portion of a normal life consider Michael Milken. Michael Milken is considered the inventor of high yield "Junk Bonds". Some people would argue the name given the benefits that have flowed from such offering since their invention in

Chapter 8. Learning Without Making Fatal Mistakes

the 1980's. Michael Milken and Ivan Boesky while enjoying a great life also made some fatal errors that got them in the middle of a fraud scandal that cost them millions of dollars and what most would consider a scandalous end to a great career. Some of this was chronicled in the New York Times on September 26, 2002 in an article entitled "Public Lives; Nearly 96, Judge Keeps an Iron Grip on the Gavel". The reason I note this article is the irony that it so clearly depicts between a Judge at age 96 who has made difficult decisions all his life and continues to succeed, while the people before him at a little more than half his age have made some fatal errors that cost them greatly. Secondly, Michael Milken despite his failings came back to become the founder of the Prostrate Cancer Foundation which was derived from his interest in medical philanthropy and his own case of prostrate cancer. He is still one of the top 500 richest people as rated by Forbes in 2007. His situation is certainly one of extreme odds, but it stands as an example for positive thinking and persistence when all else seems to have failed. Ivan Boesky has survived a difficult period himself and currently enjoys some success as he quietly supports Hillary Clinton for president according to Michael McAuliff of "The Washington Bureau" at the Daily News.

Your story is not likely to fill the pages of the New York Times, but it will always be of great importance to you. Don't underestimate the value of simple approaches to difficult problems that may seem insurmountable at the time they occur. Certainly avoidance of errors is the best approach, but knowing how to cope with adversity will always hold value even when it is rarely used.

Developing coping skills will help you make that step by step march through adverse conditions. Staying engaged in a positive effort to achieve goals or even dreams makes you available to the opportunity that may occur in an unexpected way. If instead you choose to sit on the sidelines your skills are left to deteriorate over time leaving you less prepared and generally less available to all opportunity. How many times have you heard someone say, "keep moving forward even if you fail occasionally you are apt to be in a better place tomorrow than you were today?" Staying engaged in positive effort has benefits to numerous to mention, because they tend to impact an entire circle of people.

I would like to share another experience from my days as a skydiver that tested my coping skills. I had by this time many jumps and some from altitudes as high as 15,500 feet. This was one of those high jumps where three other jumpers and I planned to do some relative work. That is to say we would jump from the plane one after the other join up and create a ring as we fell for several thousand feet.

The perspective of the others was somewhat different than mine, because they were all wearing high performance parachutes and I was not. I didn't see this difference of perspective as a problem, because I assumed they would pick the exit point based on the lowest capability parachute. Wrong!!!!! Never assume.

After a rather uneventful airplane exit, freefall and opening, I was about to experience my most difficult parachute ride ever. Upon

Chapter 8. Learning Without Making Fatal Mistakes

opening I realized I was not high enough to get over all of the power lines that lie below, due to my low performance parachute. The options were not good, because turning away from the gauntlet of wires would put me into some high trees and as I descended the option to turn diminished.

I opted to make a run over the highest wires and one secondary set of lower wires. This option required a quick turn to avoid hanging in a third set of wires. As I past only feet above the highest wires I noted that a house was downwind in what I anticipated as my landing spot. This situation was complicated by what appeared to be piles of scrap iron that surrounded the house and garage area. As I went downwind toward the house I noticed an area cleared in front of the garage door that happened to be opened.

That clearing would be my target, but would require me to pass over it and return. This strategy would enable me to avoid a forth set of wires running perpendicular to the first three sets of wires. As I made my final turn I realized I was on a trajectory that would put me into the scrap iron that was beyond the small clearing that offered a safe landing. I rationalized in the remaining seconds that the only way to avoid the scrap heap was to stall my parachute perhaps five to ten feet above the clearing.

As I stalled my parachute I hit the ground rather hard and rolled into the garage where I encountered a rather startled resident that was in the process of arc welding some of that iron from the surrounding scrap heap. Fortunately for me that is where the drama ended. He thought I was quite fortunate to avoid hitting the house, although he had to help me retrieve my parachute from the roof of his garage. Despite avoiding a panic mentality at any step along the way it was never quite clear until I got up off the ground in one piece that I would avoid making a fatal mistake.

Certainly coping when things go wrong saved the day in that extreme example, but where are the best examples in business? Some aspects of business lend themselves to the need for coping skills better than others. The salesperson is usually considered a person most likely to need coping skills on a daily basis, because sales typically have a high rate of rejection. The average office worker or production worker is not accustomed to hearing people reject them daily. Salespeople must endure constant rejection even when the customer has invited them to present their product line.

One edge that the seasoned salesperson has on the rate of rejection is that the errors that they make in any presentation are not fatal. Most salespeople are practiced presenters that realize its nothing significant or personal. The customer may just not be ready to buy. The salesperson needs to detect who is ready and who is not quickly to allow them to move on to the ready buyer quickly.

Suffering small setbacks make you more like the salesman that persists until they learn to consistently sell. People pursuing knowledge and understanding often encounter difficulty and discouragement. Therefore anyone intending to achieve mastery or competence can learn from the salesperson. One sales person stands

Chapter 8. Learning Without Making Fatal Mistakes

out in my mind, Joe Girard. "How to Sell Anything to Anybody" 1977 by Joe Girard, author Stanley H. Brown and author Robert Casemore is a best selling book by a car salesman that had achieved a very notable sales record.

Joe Girard became a salesman after failing elsewhere. What he understood was that information contained in something as simple as a telephone book could be a vehicle to his success if he would listen, learn and keep a positive attitude along the way. He certainly succeeded beyond his early expectations, but he probably set a new standard for customer care when there virtually was none. Successful students usually succeed based on patience and persistence with themselves as well as others.

Despite the changes that the automobile industry has under gone over the past 30 years Joe Girards' tips on selling are still respected and reviewed by many salespeople today. There is something to be said for a simple approach to satisfying customers that not only come back, but send their friends on a word of mouth reference. Joes' early failures were never fatal errors and he recovered quickly to go on to succeed.

Understand the risk based on your best information and use the passion of your purpose to sustain patience and persistence that will nurture your success.

CHAPTER 9

Assessing Your Status

Gaining perspective of your position relative to where you were yesterday requires that you recognize your achievement. Perspective of others, if objective, is the best indicator of where you are compared to where you were. This same view allows you to assess the position of the people around you and share your impressions with others. Biographies of other people can give you greater perspective, because their lives are reviewed in what seems like the blink of an eye. How is perspective used to unlock the value of information? Knowing where you are makes it easy to appreciate how far you have come and how much further you need to go if you are planning to do anything. If it stirs your emotions harness them and use the energy. More information will help you adjust your plans for the future.

If your definition of achievement is financial freedom you may wait a long time before you ever celebrate any success. Stop to evaluate where you are on a regular basis. Celebrate all those incremental successes on the way to financial freedom, because it will reinforce and sustain your persistence. Any step along the way is higher ground than that starting position and should be celebrated if only in a modest way. Easy to measure events are times to celebrate. Closing out a credit account, celebrate! Paying off an automobile, celebrate! Paying off school loans, celebrate! Find easy to measure steps toward your goal that give you opportunity to enjoy the work you do from day to day to get closer to some larger goal.

When you are striving to accomplish an objective or a larger goal your evaluation can be obscured by your desire to succeed. Establish some objective measurements of success ahead of any effort to succeed. You can easily use these as markers to aim for as you strive to succeed and secondly to evaluate your performance at the end of the day. The important thing is to set them ahead of the effort to avoid shaping your objectives to match your performance. If you do this in advance you are more likely to stretch to reach a mark than you are to settle for a second rate performance that you determine is good enough at the end of the day.

Perspective can be used after an event for long term management, but perhaps more rigorous rules that are reviewed ahead of any engagement will better serve the athlete or the competitor. Rules and laws are violated everyday with no consequence, but occasionally someone will violate what is called a "Law of Nature". These violations are usually penalized quickly and without consideration by another person or a court of law. The punishment for violating a Law of Nature is usually as severe as the violation.

Chapter 9. Assessing Your Status

Examples include, but are not limited to gravity. If a person does not respect the law of gravity and how it works the penalty will be exacted at 32 feet per second per second. Perspective can make us aware of big and small violations that we need to be conscious of as we are engaged in achieving our everyday objectives and goals.

As much as I am reluctant to interfere with my neighbors and their children, one day I had to get out of my comfortable seat and take action. It just so happened that the children, that were in their teens, were left home alone and had friends over for a swimming party. They were having fun diving from different points of the deck into the pool, all is well so far. The next time I look up someone is jumping off the first level roof into the pool. This got my attention. When I saw one of them working their way onto the second story roof I had to take action. I never would have forgiven myself if I just sat by and watched them risk it all for a splash into a pool. The minute I appeared and questioned what they were doing they immediately retreated from the roof, knowing they had probably gone too far. My presence and perspective on their activity at least gave some of them permission to consider alternatives and behave more responsibly than they would have with just their friends present.

Any successful person has not succeeded as a result of never having failed. Successful people succeed despite any number of failures. These failures are looked at as lessons on the way to their success. Perhaps your failures have lead to quitting. No one likes to loose consistently, but much learning includes failure as you try to apply what you have learned in a real environment outside of the classroom. Quitting only eliminates you from the competition with other people it does not improve your odds of success somewhere else.

Failure can also be a simple indication that you were wrong despite your best efforts. The persistence you bring to your effort should help you sift through mistakes made to find a winning combination. If you watch any professional sport you understand that someone wins and someone looses. The margin between winning and loosing can be very small, but that does not stop the results from being labeled either a win or a loss. Gaining approval in a business environment may be less clear cut unless you press for decisions to be made that change the status quo.

If competing in a particular field requires characteristics or traits you do not possess, or have any success at developing, the road to success is apt to be long. Although, your desire may outweigh your ability don't let your shortcomings stop you. Get an assessment from someone capable of making an objective assessment you trust. Knowing what you need to overcome and what the alternatives are is a good place to start. There may be alternate opportunities that you have not considered that are as appealing as your first consideration. Ask yourself are there other people like you that have succeeded? You may only lack patience and persistence. That unfortunately is not an unusual or easy condition to overcome. Patience and persistence of effort is developed on a moment to moment, hour by hour, day by day and year by year basis. If you discover this is a part of the failure you have experienced start by learning something about people that have succeeded despite failure.

Look for examples of successful people in your own life first, because they are most available to you and may be able to give you some of the best first hand advise. A person I met, only over the telephone, that was very helpful to me is probably someone who may never remember me. Her name is Temple Grandin. I first learned of her as I was driving home from work and heard her being interviewed on the radio some twelve years ago.

My first reaction to her interview was, how could this person persevere through the trials she faced to her remarkable level of achievement? As I continued to listen to her, she described some of her friends and acquaintances that struggled similarly to be part of what others regarded as a normal life. Among those she referenced was a woman that did remarkable computer programming. Her friend didn't get a lot of high visibility, because she would come in late at night and leave early before others arrived. She like Temple shared what we have come to know as Autism.

Temple went on to describe how her friend could find some of the most elegant solutions probably, because they both tended to solve problems from a different perspective. Temple described her thought process as "Thinking Like a Cow" which was rephrased by someone helping her write her first book to "Thinking in Pictures". To understand this you need to know that Temple Grandin is world renowned for designing cattle handling equipment world wide,

Chapter 9. Assessing Your Status

because she has probably designed or influenced the design of one third of all cattle handling equipment in this country. After thinking a design through she could virtually do a walk through in her mind to make corrections before putting it down on paper.

Being a tooling designer myself and currently struggling to improve a rather complicated data management system I was investigating I needed to know more. I bought her book "Thinking in Pictures" and read it almost non-stop. Visualizing her designs from the cows' perspective seemed to make the most significant difference in her approach. If that was true perhaps I could take a different perspective to solve some of the programming problems I was experiencing.

I began to consider the information retrieval process that was so cumbersome that some queries for information took several hours. As the programming began to take shape the queries took less and less time. Some of those longest queries now took only thirty seconds. I was sold! I looked up Temple Grandin, she was an Associate Professor at Colorado State University. I called that day and left a message thanking her for her contribution to my efforts. Remarkably, she called back and we had a conversation that could only be described as one between old friends. She remarked that, "she does seem to achieve a very good connection with engineers." I told her that the life experience she shared changed my perspective on problem solving that will improve my performance in the future evermore.

That year I shared this story with many of my friends and

neighbors always ending it with the quip "Think like a cow" and not surprisingly I was the benefactor of much cow paraphernalia. All that year I was showered with cow statuettes, cow print hats, a cow print robe and finally cow shaped Christmas lights. Even when you are accomplishing serious objectives and goals you can still have fun. Don't let the pursuit of the achievement grind you down instead find a way to enjoy the journey every step of the way.

When you go about living your life everyday and have a small circle of friends you tend to loose sight of the big picture. How can you expand your horizon? Understanding how fortunate a life you have lead can be driven home by the experiences of other people. A person that I have never had the pleasure to meet, but has lived a life that should give anybody encouragement when it comes to overcoming adversity and achievement is Monty Roberts.

After seeing a brief story on television about his ability to communicate with horses I bought his book, "The Man Who Listens to Horses." His amazing skill that he claims he can teach people is not nearly as amazing as his life story to gain recognition by his father and other people in the horse training business. He persisted against all odds and succeeded on a world wide stage.

The demonstration of his skill that launched a career that until then was modest was his demonstration before the Queen of England at age 59. Even if his achievement comes a little late in life, anyone that reads his story will be encouraged to persist in a quest to achieve what might only seem like a distant dream.

Chapter 9. Assessing Your Status

The story of his trials began while he was a young boy and persisted into his adult life. A lifetime of overcoming obstacles that were a part of his life can give others some perspective when considering the challenges they face as they reach for success.

As I recall these extreme examples of success I am reminded of the many examples of success of not so famous people I personally know. No less than a half dozen people come to mind. Their lives are more like mine than are those reported by the media. Like those reported in the media they to have achieved goals despite the difficulties they have encountered.

I am sure that if you consider your family, friends, associates and even those people that you occasionally see in your community you will find many that have worked out of the spotlight to achieve a better day tomorrow. Let their effort be an example for the effort you need to apply to succeed.

One remote example that I witnessed the other day occurred while my wife and I were visiting my mother-in-law at her assisted living facility. While we were sitting in the parlor visiting, a woman came through the door with a gentleman in a wheelchair. We greeted them as they sat down next to another woman and began to visit.

Later as we were about to leave they said they needed to get going as well, because another family member was in the adjacent building that they needed to visit. It occurred to me that this one seemingly well woman had responsibility for taking her husband in a

Chapter 9. Assessing Your Status

wheelchair to visit his mother in the assisted living facility and visit her own mother there as well. It certainly made my visit seem simple.

Every time I see this couple from this day forward I will be reminded how easy my lot in life is. A person would almost need to where blinders or dark glasses to avoid seeing the many examples of how ordinary people deal with extraordinary circumstances. I am not discouraged by what I see, but encouraged that most people can do more than they feel they are capable of doing.

Managing your emotions is important if you hope to stay rational. When we are emotional it tends to cloud our thinking. If you are emotional when you need to be thinking it can be a rather chaotic experience. I do not suggest you suppress your emotion just use it wisely. Emotion can give you that extra adrenaline you need to be first rather than second. Knowing when to let your emotions flow can be tricky. The same emotion that will propel you to first place can be the energy behind the intolerable foul. If you doubt this watch any athlete as they struggle to manage their emotions throughout any competition. Fouls committed in business and personal life may be less forgiving than the sports arena that manages fouls on a regular basis.

If your perspective anticipates emotional moments it should allow you to prepare to harness the energy that surrounds any emotional event. Some sports figures will use a minor injury to either draw a foul by dramatic behavior or enable them to bounce to their feet and perform at a higher level. Channeling the energy of your

Chapter 9. Assessing Your Status

emotions can be a very valuable tool. The information that informs you of that opportunity is your perspective before during and after an event.

You will have greater opportunity to plan for how you may use what until now may have been wasted energy. Being energy conscious is more than driving a high mileage vehicle. If you were being drained by other frustrating events consider the energy value they may have if you made a focused effort to direct that energy into some productive activity.

CHAPTER 10

The Frontier

The frontier fortunately is a familiar landscape regardless of your choice of work. It is what it always has been, a struggle to use the ever present inherent abilities you have always had to slice and dice large pieces of information into small meaningful nuggets that have value. The work of preparing is made easier knowing you are already equipped. The gadgets announced at the latest Consumers Electronics Show may give you new ways to access and manage information, but extracting value will still be your task. Extracting value from a mountain of information still comes down to the individual and their commitment.

What you might address when considering the frontier is your preparedness to engage it as people have in the past. Although there may not be a school that specializes in training people for the frontiers of life, consider what basic skills you currently have along with a fitness to engage life without an instruction book. Can you break down information? Can you work in an adverse environment? Can

Chapter 10. The Frontier

you make decisions? If you have basic skills and a passion to succeed then consider the map you have for success. A map is a plan for success that is never perfect, but always indispensible. Maps for early explorers and frontier people were used when available, but not relied on for detail.

Today the frontier for me is the world of finance. Although my interest comes late in life, the last 15 years, the passion I have for it is not diminished. I spend countless hours engaging the world in a competition for some portion of that pile of cash that sloshes around everyday in every country in the world. Billions and trillions of dollars are moved everyday in the markets of the world, and today anyone with the ability to reach the internet can be a player. It is an area where information and your decision making process is critical to your success.

A remarkable volume of money comes and goes daily without seeming to change the way people conduct their lives day by day. A single example of this was the fraudulent behavior of one commodity trader at a bank in Europe. It may have missed your notice, but this single trader that was detected in January of 2008 mishandled seven billion dollars. Some have speculated that volume of money may impact as much as 50 billion dollars in investments, AFP 2008 (http://sg.news.yahoo.com/afp/20080209/tts-france-banking-societegenerale-crime-509a08e.html).

More significant volumes of money move without notice everyday in the currency markets. 3.2 trillion dollars in currency

Chapter 10. The Frontier

is traded daily as reported by the Finfacts Team in December 2007 (http://www.finfacts.com/irelandbusinessnews/publish/article_1011278 .shtml). With the growth of foreign markets namely India and China that number could grow to 5 trillion dollars in the next few years. Dabbling in these markets is not for the faint hearted, because fortunes are lost as quickly as they are gained.

Despite the numerous maps to success only a small percentage of people succeed at currency trading. A far greater number of people with less ambitious goals achieve remarkable success investing world wide. Although working long and hard and collecting a pension is an honorable thing to do, it probably is not the most likely path for young people today. Young people today are making money a different way, through investment, money management and over the internet in the financial centers of the world that are virtually open twenty four hours a day six days a week.

The challenges of the future will rely on leaders that know how to take information that may be sitting in plain sight, but until now not used to make a difference in the everyday world we live in. The leaders of tomorrow are those extraordinary people that move heaven and earth to get to where they are going. They sense the answers they need are always within their reach.

Leaders that have a long list of credentials may not succeed unless the credentials they have achieved have given them that experience of having to work in a somewhat lonely environment. Self-reliance is an indispensible trait that is not easily developed.

Chapter 10. The Frontier

Most higher education tends to wean the individual from personal support making them either more independent individuals or more dependent on networks of friends and classmates to study with as they try to distill the important information that will enable them to rationalize larger questions that they will be tested on. Even though most students become both more independent and more appreciative of networks, the danger is that some students will always look for the shortcut or easy way to get the understanding they need. What they fail to understand is that the process used to legitimately find the answers is the same process that will be needed on the frontier where shortcuts and stepping around the process is not possible.

Gadgetry may help gather greater amounts of information, but the decision you make will be based on how you weigh the options you have considered. Using gadgetry may help calculate the probabilities that influence you, but no ownership will be assumed by the hardware bought off the shelf. As the owner you will need to be clear as to the direction that money and effort will be directed.

Today there is no single frontier instead there are countless opportunities that exist for people that want a challenge. The advantage of the volume of information and sources of information is that it gives every person with the freedom to pursue it a place to start. You can do much more examination of the possibilities than was available in the past.

As you stand on the edge of a frontier the person that has prepared themselves for it will be energized by the challenge instead of complacent or frightened. Frontiers have existed since the beginning of time, but today you can be pursue them from the privacy of your home, a field in the wilderness, or from an office tower. Collaboration can be done from any of these locations with virtually anyone else in the world.

There are fewer barriers today than there have ever been in the past, but the question still remains. Are you ready? Can you sift through information and separate the value that can be recycled as another product or service? Will other people recognize that ability in you as an individual? How have you demonstrated your ability in the past? What do you plan to do that will continue to strengthen your natural talents?

If your goal is to climb Mt Everest there are experienced teams that can help you realize your dream, but as you near the summit it will be your commitment and your decision to go forward or to head back. Here again you own your destiny. You and you alone will need to make what might be life and death decisions. The effort spent in such an adventure will not be quick or inexpensive and preparation will determine what team is willing to guide your effort.

If your goal is to go to a university there are counselors and schools willing to contribute to your effort. Of course the first thing they are going to want to know is how have you prepared for the adventure? Does the effort you have made in the past give them some assurance that you can succeed over four years? Here again it will not be quick or inexpensive and preparation will determine what schools

Chapter 10. The Frontier

accept you and are willing to contribute to your effort.

If your goal is to escape from debt that stifles your ability to do much more than pay the minimum payment every month there are financial advisors that can help you develop a plan. They of course are going to want to know what you have been doing in small ways to diminish your debt. What preparation have you done to live a less expensive life style? Have you demonstrated that you can deny yourself luxury items or that you are willing to work longer hours to reduce your debt? Once again it will take time and greater effort to get out of debt than it took to get into debt, but are you ready? They will assure you that you own the debt and the ability to reduce it. If they are to improve your life, it will take your involvement.

If your goal is to clear, clean and organize your room, house or garage, a lofty goal for some a way of life for others, it will depend on you. No one person can do for you what you will not plan and make happen for yourself unless you reside in an assisted living facility. Not living in an institution means that you have free will and are subject to the good and bad behavior you have established in the past. To improve a deteriorating circumstance takes your accepting ownership for what you need to do to make a difference. Outside services are temporary fixes that are not likely to change bad habits of the past. So calling a cleaning service may not be the answer unless they are called frequently evermore. Instead it will depend on you to make the plan and to carry it out over time developing better habits as you achieve your goal.

Chapter 10. The Frontier

Goals big and small will always require consideration of certain information. Learn to engage the information with your natural talents that do not require a trip to the electronics store. Unlocking the value of that information will take some practice and time to achieve, so start today.

Your goals may take you in a direction that no one person can identify today, but the need for you to engage the world and consider information will still be a common thread between us. Don't shrink from the challenge stand up to the flow of information and let it wash over you. Through your defiant quest to find value in information you will move into the future with confidence.

www.ingramcontent.com/pod-product-compliance
Lightning Source LLC
Chambersburg PA
CBHW021143070326
40689CB00043B/1016